Best wishes
Joyce [illegible]

Joyce Cosme-Collis

Acknowledgement

I thank my husband Felix Cosme for all the support he has contributed for the success of this book.

Thanks go to friends and relations who have sent me photographs of recent times, and of days gone by.

Sadly my cousin John Price has passed away since I started on this book, he has sent me his paintings of India, he would have been very pleased to see them in a book.

Joyce Cosme-Collis

Joyce Cosme-Collis

Around The World In 80 Years

Published 2009

ISBN 978-0-9563324-1-7

Jacket front: Joyce with her Bearded Collies on the Vetzyme advertising shoot

Jacket back: Joyces daughter Carol with her husband Neil in front of the Taj Mahal

Published by Felix Cosme

Typeset in 11 on 13 point Bookman
Designed and produced by Rivers Media Services Limited
Brockington Studio, Bodenham, Herefordshire HR1 3HT
Printed and bound by Cromwell Press Group, Trowbridge, Wiltshire

CONTENTS

George Ernest Stone married to Kathleen Howard

INTRODUCTION

MY father was born in Cork, Ireland, in 1900, where his father was stationed in the Army. My mother was born in Kent 1901. I can imagine a very different way of life was theirs as they grew up. My father came from a generation of Military ancestors, so it was not surprising that he would have joined the Army when he was 16.

My mothers life was very different, in fact shrouded in mystery. I was taught from an early age not to ask questions, and to call my grandmother 'Auntie Flossie', and my great grandmother 'Auntie Vincent', and her husband 'Uncle Vincent', I was glad there would never be a reason for me to address him as I was terrified of him, especially when he gave me a sharp look. I learnt later that he had owned his own sailing ship and used it to transport slaves from the West coast of Africa to the East coast of America. Auntie Vincent was a lady like, sweet-tempered person, soft spoken and of a nervous disposition. How she happened to be married to such a frightening man must have surprised everyone they met.

I had very little idea of either my mother or my father's early life, or how their paths crossed, other than my father was stationed in the Barracks in Crowborough, the village where my mother lived with Auntie Vincent and Uncle Vincent. This would be the time when both the old couple had retired, and owned a Post Office. My parents were married in July 1920, my brother was born in 1922, and I was born in July 1923 in Kent.

Our life from the very beginning taught us to accept the Army life without complaint. It was unlikely the complaint would be dealt with in our favour, in fact, a complaint from either of us, at any time would have shocked our parents. My father was so used to giving orders and always expected them to be obeyed immediately. My mother was brought up by Victorian grand-parents who were also extremely strict. My parents favourite saying was “Children should be seen but never heard”. Peter my brother was a very good looking little boy, admired by everyone.

I was shy, very shy. I learnt my lesson on how to behave when I went shopping with my mother at a very early age. We were in a Grocery store, and I asked for some sweets, when my mother was talking to a friend. I should have remembered “Children should be seen but not heard”. My mother was annoyed and dragged me outside of the shop, where there was a horse trough, she dunked my head in the water and said, “Let that be a lesson to you, don’t ever interrupt when I am talking”. Both my brother and I were well dressed, well looked after, and well fed by two very strict parents. Until we left for India we had a lady looking after us, and when we arrived in India we had an ayah, neither of them were strict, so our life was evened out with kind love.

Right: My Great Grandmother Auntie Vincent & Great Grandfather Uncle Vincent

Below: Uncle Vincent outside his house

George Ernest Stone in Russia 1919

On parade in India

THE EARLY DAYS
LIFE IN INDIA

MY father was a young soldier in the British Army, when he was nineteen years old he was sent to Russia with his regiment. The 1914-18 war was on, we and the Russians were at war with Germany. When that war ended my father returned to Crowborough Barracks. His next overseas move was expected to do a tour of duty as his regiment was needed in 1927 in India.

My mother was not too happy about taking my brother and I to India in those early days. She had heard all sorts of rumours that were circulated about the Spartan conditions that the service men and their families were expected to cope with. Families who became so depleted by the death of one or two of their children were sent home in sympathy before others of the family died. She had heard that the childhood diseases that were only cause for minor concern in Great Britain were killers in that hot country. Stories of children dying of Dysentery, snake bites, scorpion stings, and overcome by the heat, so it was no wonder that my mother was worried.

Our sailing day was booked on the troop ship HMS Navasa, for November 1927 and the only bright spot was that we would not have to endure another cold winter, we would be in the heat and sun of the Indian plains. The unknown situations that could arise with two very small children in that distant country had to be accepted, and also the ship voyage that offered very little comfort, and less amenities must be endured so that my mother could be with her husband for six years, the length of his stay.

I do not remember very much about the journey, but my brother was into mischief most of the time, and the rest of the voyage he was being seasick. It seemed a very slow journey and by the time we landed in Bombay we had adjusted to the heat. The new arrivals were sent to Jabalpur in the Central plains of India. At first we had to live in huge tents, as the families who had finished their tour of duty were due to go back home, but had not left their home in the Barracks. HMS Navasa was in dry dock for a month before the next contingent of soldiers and their families arrived to make their journey home to Great Britain.

One day while living in the tents my parents woke me up to ask what had happened to my blanket that was on my bed when I had gone to sleep. I had no answer for them, I had not missed it from my bed. They looked further in the different compartments of the tents and noticed several other things missing. The fruit bowl was empty, different kitchen utensils had gone, and as they continued their search they realized that we had been robbed during the night. When the police soldiers came they told us this was a usual occurrence when new arrivals came and had to live in tents. The Indian robbers stripped naked, covered their body with oil, so if they got caught they could not be held. They would have taken the blanket from my bed. If I had woken up the whole Barrack compound would have been alerted when they heard my screams. I was so frightened to go to sleep the next night, that I wanted to return to England. Surprisingly my mother did not chastise me for crying.

We were all so pleased when it came about that we were allocated a beautiful house, with a private garden and a huge verandah. Behind the house was a covered passage leading to the kitchen where all the utensils and large oven was ready for our cook who was to work for us.

The barracks was sprawled out over several acres of

HMS Troopship Navasa the ship that we travelled to India on

My mother Kathleen Stone, Peter and myself with our servants living in a tent as we had just arrived in Jabalpur

Peter & Joyce

Our cook outside the new cook houses being built in the Barracks

land, housing the Royal Corps of Signals, my fathers regiment, and the Artillery Regiment. The children from both had to attend the one school. We had to be at school at 7.30 am and we finished at 12 noon as it was too hot to do anything other than sleep in the afternoon. The hospital, prison and main buildings had to serve all the families belonging to the service men. Right in the centre of the Barracks was the mess hall, the meeting place for everyone. That is where the post arrived, also the rations for the families had to be collected from there. Special holidays, like Christmas and other days were celebrated with the whole family allowed into the grounds. Mainly the mess hall was for the service men where they enjoyed their time for relaxation playing billiards and cards.

Christmas was spent with a huge party, where everyone joined in the festivities. The highlight of the day was a ride on an elephant, and father Xmas coming down a makeshift chimney with a huge sack of toys. Xmas was one of the hottest days in the middle of the Indian summer, which took many of us a little time adjusting to. There was a regular change over of families coming in from England, and then returning after their time was completed. Many of the families brought their pets with them when they came to India as there was no quarantine for their dogs, sadly when they returned back to England they either abandoned their dogs with no thought for their welfare, just leaving them to fend for themselves, or passing them on to families that would be staying longer. It soon became the survival of the fittest, and the pack of pedigree dogs soon became a pack of mongrel dogs. The pedigree dogs brought from England did not have the stamina to withstand the rigours of living wild and soon succumbed to disease, unfortunately leaving behind them litters of unwanted half wild puppies.

When the pack of wild dogs caused too much trouble the authorities would send the soldiers to shoot on sight any dog seen running loose. That is when we made sure our house dogs were securely locked up, as we later had a mongrel bitch that had been left by its owners when they returned to England.

It was one of these dogs that came regularly to our verandah to steal food. He was only half wild and was not so frightened of humans when it was chased away, in fact it would often stand its ground and snarl in defiance, before it reluctantly gave in and cringed away. This dog eventually had suspected rabies, and in that terrible state it came to our place for water. I was playing alone on the verandah my ayah (nanny) was in the house, and my parents had gone to the Bazaar. I shouted at the dog and lifted my arm as if I was going to throw something at it, it lunged at me and bit my wrist then ran off. The wound was painful and bleeding profusely, a soldier neighbour who was passing by, rushed me to the hospital where I was immediately put in isolation. A doctor let my wound

We spent Christmases at the Prices home, 9 Gurudwara Road, New Dehli.
Illustration by the late John Price

When we arrived in Dehli the first time we were taken here to Safdar Jang Tomb

Christmas celebration in Jabalpur

My mother, Peter and me on the verandah of the new house

My Dad and Mum with friends

bleed for some time then cauterised it. I was given several injections then shut up in a room alone for some time. My Parents were allowed to visit me but I was not allowed to mix with anyone else, other than the nurse and the doctor for three whole weeks. Each day I was given a very painful injection in my stomach. During that time, I did not know it until late, the soldiers were sent out to catch the dog so that they could take saliva test from it, the doctor insisted that it be brought in alive so that positive test could be made. Unfortunately the soldier who saw the dog panicked and shot it dead. I must have been one of the lucky ones and survived the dreaded disease, or the dog did not have rabies as at first suspected. I was too young to really panic, but my parents were really worried.

This did not put me off the canine breed, and when my mother took in a mongrel type of Collie that had been left behind by its previous owners I was overjoyed.

My parents were not dog lovers to any extent, but they were sorry for the bitch and did not want her to join the pack of wild dogs. Lady was allowed to roam around the Barracks, that did not matter when she was a puppy, but before long she became interesting to the dogs in the area and they came visiting. With no idea of what might happen my parents allowed Lady to continue with her freedom, and even when she was attended to by several males they thought nothing of it. Needless to say 63 days later Lady produced six mixed type puppies. I loved everyone of them, I threw away my dolls and put the puppies in my dolls pram. I spent more time with that litter than the mother was allowed to, who had seen my pleasure and interest in her offspring and went away seeking her own pleasures, leaving me to be nurse maid. Surprisingly the puppies thrived even after they were taken everywhere in my pram. It was a good thing that I was sensible enough to allow the mother to have access to them every so often to feed them, but I also spent hours supplementing their meal with milk and honey served from my doll's bottle. When the time came for them to be given away I could not believe that my mother would be so heartless. To me they were my six little brothers and sisters, I wanted to keep them forever. My world was turned upside down when they went, not only were they given away, but Lady was in whelp again so was put to sleep. The pack of amorous dogs were forever camping out on our verandah looking for Lady. "Filthy animals and spreading disease," my mother complained.

For weeks I went into mourning until my mother could stand it no longer, this coincided with her win at a Whist drive. She went regularly to the mess hall and was very lucky winning several prizes. This time she won a bottle of spirits, and as a non drinker she offered to exchange her prize with the person who won an 8 week old Scottish Terrier puppy. She bought it home, it was in a basket with a cover over the top and a huge red bow tied around the basket, I did not know what she was giving me. When I opened the basket and saw that very sweet black bundle of fluff, with tiny blackberry eyes gazing up at me I burst out crying with joy. We called him Barloo, which is Hindustani for Black Bear. I loved him dearly, and with such lavish and loving attention he developed the most wonderful character. I remember his antics to amuse my guests at one of my birthday parties. He put his head in a shopping basket and ran around with it on his head, the children's laughter encouraged him to do even more funny antics.

Poor Barloo had many unhappy experiences too. If my family had been out for the evening and we came home into the dark house Barloo was encouraged to go into the rooms first, so he could frighten any snakes away. This particular evening it was not a snake that had taken refuge in our house, but a scorpion, and Barloo immediately attacked it before we could come to his rescue. He worried it but had sense enough to back away each time it raised its sting.

But he became so excited and before my father had time to light the lamps (there was no electricity at that time in the Barracks) the scorpion had stung Barloo on the nose. He yelped then dashed past us out into the night. For days we hunted for him but with no success. Our Indian cook said we were not to worry, he knew that dogs born in India would know what plants to eat to counteract the scorpion or snake venom. I don't know if that was correct but after eight days Barloo came home, he was very thin, and his nose had lost its pigment, we made such a fuss of him and he lapped up this special treatment and soon settled down to sleep. Barloo's next escapade was very upsetting, one of his main interests in life was to chase the monkeys that came into the compound to steal food. The same family of monkeys would sit in the trees shrieking at him, teasing him they would come down to the lowest branches of the tree, then scream at him and climb higher as he jumped for them, they must have sensed that he was not playing in fact if he could have caught one of them he would have killed it.

We tried desperately to stop him whenever we could. One day a soldier came to speak to my father, and as he came to the door Barloo saw a monkey had come down to the verandah, with a swift lunge he nearly caught it, but it jumped onto the soldier's back and clung tightly to his neck with his dirty claws. In the heat the soldier was only in an open neck shirt, his neck was scratched badly. Needless to say the poor man was rushed off to the hospital, and Barloo was in disgrace again, he was house bound for several days.

We found him barking and scratching at a hole under the verandah, a passerby was sure he had seen a large green snake go into the hole. Everyone crowded around and suggested ways of getting the snake out of the hole. Eventually it was decided to smoke it out and lighted rags were stuffed into the hole. It was rather a shame that the smoke found its way into our sitting room, but my mother, although rather house proud, said she would put up with that so long as the venomous snake was brought out and killed. By this time an even larger crowd had collected and all waited for the result of the dense smoke to produce the results. Heavy sticks and even a gun was held at the ready. Movement was sighted and we all stood back, then out crawled a large badly burned green toad. It would not have harmed anyone. Again Barloo was in disgrace especially as my mother had to get the laundry man to wash the curtains and chair covers from the sitting room, although the smell of smoke stayed with us for days afterwards.

Barloo developed a dislike of Indians, which was rather a problem as we were living in India. He would lay quietly on the verandah in the dark and watch for the Indian servants who left the Barracks to go home to the Back Bazaar where they lived. He knew which one would shout and scream at him and the nervous ones who would run for their lives, and he chose those to chase. The servants who had sticks to ward him off he left alone. How he knew the difference in the dark puzzled us until we realized that the Indian women wore bells on their ankles attached to their feet bracelets to frighten away the snakes that might lay in their path. We left school at 12.30pm, had tiffin (lunch) then we were supposed to lay on our beds during the heat of the day. We were two very active children and often crept out while our parents slept. Sometimes we went to the Fox Hound Kennels.

Peter and I were getting to really enjoy our life in Jabalpur, my mother was also enjoying the life. My father had been promoted and she spent more time playing tennis and spending most of her evenings in the Mess playing cards with her friends. We had an Ahaja who stayed on guard with us while our parents were away.

We were free to enjoy the wide open spaces around the

My Dad shot the Panther hanging on the lounge

Peter and me at our stables

A notice that was sent to all homes about a new shoe shop opening

NOTICE.

The Undersigned Have Opened A

CHINA FOOT WEAR HOUSE

IN

No. 64, EAST STREET, SADAR BAZAR,

JUBBULPORE.

We guarantee best finish and entire satisfaction with Moderate Prices.

A trial order will convince the customers and solicit. Kind Gentlemen and Ladies will be pleased to patronize our new foot wear shop and test our ability, and place orders on satisfying our best material, good finish and low rate of prices charged, than any in the market foot wear shops stationed in Jubbulpore.

Our appeal to the public of Jubbulpore to be kind enough to favour us with their presence once and test our workmanship and favour us the newly established China Foot Wear House for all we are worth.

We are

Yours faithfully,

YOUNG CHONG & Co.

Proprietors of

CHINA FOOT WEAR HOUSE,

No. 64, East Street, Sadar Bazar,

JUBBULPORE.

Shubh Chintak Press, Jubbulpore.

John Price my cousin painted these Elephants for me before he died

Barracks, the whole area was our playground, there were no restrictions such as dangerous roads to cross. We got to know the whole area so well, and never got lost. We knew what time my father came home, when he was not away with his regiment, and my mother was often otherwise busy chasing the staff and cook and his family. They came every time they thought no one was at home so they could steal food or anything that was lying around.

Peter and I spent a lot of time in the Sudar Bazaar, especially when there was a religious ceremony taking place. I loved to see the elephants decorated, they looked magnificent with the painted cloths and jewellery spread over their huge bodies, they seemed to enjoy the extra attention. We were made very welcome by the celebrating crowd, and given highly coloured sweets, and jalabies to eat. When we went home to dinner it was not surprising that we had no appetite. This was the first sign of illness to my mother so she panicked and the next day she kept us back from school.

As I have mentioned before we only had to attend school from seven thirty to twelve noon. We came home from school had lunch, then everyone was expected to sleep through the hottest part of the day, until the weather became cooler.

We spent our time enjoying our freedom watching fascinated the variety of brightly coloured birds. I begged Peter not to shoot them with his gun or catapult. We also watched the black kites diving for the food we tempted them with. I noticed that there were no birds in sight until we sat on the verandah eating our lunch then flocks came from nowhere diving to snatch the food from our plates.

As soon as any food was about we were sure that the monkeys would join in the scavenging they were not my favourite animals, we had been warned that a bite or a scratch from them was very dangerous it could end up with us in hospital. This was when Peter was most busy with his catapult and rifle. At first the noise from the rifle frightened the monkeys away, they soon returned but I was always pleased when his shot missed and they were able to get away.

Whenever possible we went to the stables to ride the mules. The staff always made us welcome as we helped clean and groom the mules. The officers had their own horses at the stables when they were off duty or not being sent to different parts of India to quell an uprising. They took the opportunity to ride their horses with the hounds from the kennels.

The officers returned after quelling the trouble they had been sent to and took the opportunity to relax. We watch them ride away enviously, it was a wonderful sight to see.

The riders and hounds frightened any wild animals who crossed their path.

The sad thing was we had got to know the horses and mule's by names and we knew as they got to a certain age they would be slaughtered and taken in to the jungle where wild animals would scramble for their carcasses.

Life in the Barracks was so different there was something going on all the time. We heard that several of the horses had reached a ripe old age, and rather than see them deteriorate further, they were taken into the jungle to be shot. This attracted the wild animals so my brother, being the eldest of us youngsters, suggested that we all go to the jungle to watch the panthers and jackals eat the carcasses. My brother was 9 years old at that time and had been given another rifle for Christmas, he was so keen to use it. We set off and seemed to walk many miles with no sign of wild animals, we were also very tired, and a little worried about our parents anger for being away so long. My brother climbed the tree to see which direction we should take back to the Barracks. The younger ones

My dad searching the train at Jabalpur station

My mother, Peter and me in the garden at Jabalpur

George Stone my father at Xmas in Dehli

My mother in India

started to cry when he said he could not see any signs of the houses.

The sun goes down and in a few minutes it is dark in the central plains of India. It was such a relief when we saw flashing lights and heard shouts in the distance. At first we received a warm welcome from our rescuers then we were all chastised. My poor brother received the worst punishment as soon as we arrived home as he was the oldest. None of us suffered too much, we were tired, our feet badly blistered, but my brother had drunk from a stream, and the next day he was rushed to the hospital with Dysentery. He was very ill and not expected to live as had been the fate of so many children. His strong stamina pulled him through. But we all decided that we would not make another trip on our own to the jungle.

We did not mind going to school for 4½ hours each day as it left us plenty of free time to enjoy ourselves. Just before the darkness set in we were called in by my mother to

Mother, Peter and Joyce on Verandah, Jabalpur

The Snake Charmer

have our bath before going to bed. Our bathroom was very sparse just one chair and a cemented corner was built of bricks which was the bath. Their was a hole for the water to go out, but it had to be covered with wire netting so no snakes etc., could travel up into the bathroom. It was only by chance in certain parts of the year the tap produced clean water, usually it was very muddy coloured especially during the monsoon season. We were all excited when it did start raining especially as red cushion beetles crawled out of the ground. Millions of these beetles made the ground look as if it had a red carpet over it. Before the ground became brittle again they disappeared until the following monsoon season.

Not many of the parents were pleased when the Snake charmer was allowed to come into the Barracks compound. Their complaint was the pipe that he played to the Cobra that made them rise out of the basket would attract any other snakes in the vicinity to come into the compound. In fact this did happen, snakes came more often after the snake charmer had left.

The excited children crowded around, fascinated to see the Cobra swaying to the music, when it struck out at the pipe they all shouted out and backed away.

The snake charmer came sometimes twice in a year and expected to get money thrown in his basket.

Another visitor for money was the Indian with his dancing bear. The poor bedraggled animal with a collar and chain around his neck drew quite a lot of money from everyone that came to watch, hoping that the money would be put towards food for the bear. He stood on his hind legs and shuffled to and fro to the music. It was not a pretty sight, the officials did not send the man and his bear away, because his only income was the money he got from the Army families. I dread to imagine what sort of accommodation the poor bear had to live in.

Whenever we could we went to the swimming baths. It

was a huge building built of stone, with stairs going down into the water each end. I enjoyed sitting on the steps, with my feet in the water, but would not go any further as the water was usually green, swimming was out of the question for me, no one had any idea how often the pool was cleaned, but many adults did take a chance and survived.

We hoped one day to arrive and see the bottom of the baths, or hear that they had found a body in the murky depths and the poor soul had a proper funeral.

It was very difficult to know the different religions in India. My mother was very particular about the cook we had to prepare our food. She quite often went into the very hot cookhouse if there was any chance that the cook was allowing his family to live in the cookhouse.

She insisted that the cook have a clean cloth or serviette to bring in our dinner, he had to have it over his arm so that he could hold our plates of food. One day she caught the cook blowing into it to clean his nose. Needless to say he was immediately sacked.

One cook had a different religion. I was playing with my toys at the back door, the cook had brought his dinner out to the step, and had not noticed me, all of a sudden he let out a shout, my shadow had crossed his plate of dinner, he threw it away and complained bitterly that I should not have been there and his dinner was ruined. This was another of the religions that we had not heard about. The surprise was his food came out of the same cooking pot, as that on our plates, and which he had cooked. My mother warned me to keep away from the kitchen when food was being cooked, but she did also say “I shall never understand these Indians”. As a child I agreed with her, there were so many religions to understand.

After months of drought we welcomed the rain it went on for days and days. At first we ran out with few clothes on and revelled in the marvellous feeling of rain on our bodies. After a week with storms, lightening and thunder everyone was complaining that it was like being back in Blighty. The year that our house was hit by lightening when part of the wall tumbled down and half the roof in the night we all decided that perhaps it was not such a wonderful place to be living in.

The servants all came to help us move our furniture to the new house. It was larger than the last house with a lot more garden, and bigger verandah. The following year when the monsoon started, we did not sleep peacefully in our beds, in fact we all got up to be dressed ready, in case the lightening struck this house also.

One very upsetting day was when my father had to go before the officials in court. He had been walking towards the Bazaar with a friend when he saw a bullock had fallen to the ground and got tangled up in the reins of the cart he was pulling. The driver was whipping the bullock and shouting at it. He then took straw from the cart and set it alight then placed it under the belly of the animal to get it to stand. My father could not stand by and see such cruelty so he knocked the driver down and put out the flames. He gently got the bullock to stand and then told the driver in Hindustani that he did not want to see him doing that again. The officials warned my father never to interfere. My dad was sent to another Barracks for a month.

My brother Peter and I descended from a long line of military ancestors who had Army in their blood. So it was not surprising that he listened avidly to every word my father told him about World War One. My father was just seventeen when he volunteered to serve in the Army in 1917, he was sent to Russia, but was quite disappointed when the war ended in 1918. He was a regular soldier so returned to the barracks in Crowborough, and there he met my mother who lived in a very pretty village near the barracks.

I must admit Peter was not a kind brother, my mother told me he resented my arrival from the very beginning.

She heard me crying in my pram and found Peter had been feeding me with brown boot polish, I was being very sick so she rushed me off to hospital.

When our family moved to India in 1928 I was very wary of upsetting my brother especially around the time when he was given an air rifle for Christmas, after he shot a young girl in the arm my father took the rifle away from him.

It was not possible for Peter to be long without some sort of weapon, especially with all the animals, snakes, birds and bugs around us, so he made two catapults and was out on safari again. I remember one day he was angry because my father had criticized him for being cruel, so he went out and shot a chameleon with his catapult, it lay on the ground so Peter told me to pick it up by the tail. Of course I obeyed, thinking the poor animal was dead, but it was only stunned, and curled its body around my arm. I was terrified and dropped it and let it run away.

During the monsoon season our large house was hit by lightning again and the whole wall at the side of the house came down, we had to move into a small house while our home was being rebuilt. Peter and I had to share a bedroom and I had to put up with the dead monkey, and insects that he had collected, there was a syrup tin full of very angry wasps, I could hear the buzzing at night. Every so often he would open the lid and let them fly out, there was also a live scorpion in a large jar, a chameleon in my doll's house and a box of lizards that he had collected to see how long it would take before they grew their tails again.

My father's tour of duty was coming to an end, we had been in India for just over 6 years and plans were being made to return to England in December. We had no intentions of leaving Barloo in the care of anyone, in case he was passed on and eventually let to run wild with the packs of wild dogs. We were really upset and what had to be done dampened all our spirits for days before we sailed. I must have guessed what was to happen but could not believe that we would not take him with us. In fact a friend was asked to shoot him as soon as our family left the country, there were no Vets to peacefully put him to sleep. The long journey in the train across the plains seemed endless, my father had planned to visit our relations again in Delhi. My aunt and uncle had three children, Rupert, John and Thelma, they all made us so welcome. It was Christmas time.

The last time that we had visited them we were left with the servants while all the adults went on a visit to the Taj Mahal. I have always regretted I did not get the opportunity of being able to visit that magnificent building, so hoped it would be included in our visit this time. As we were older, my brother Peter was 12 and I was 11, we were invited to join in several parties and visited a beautiful place called Marble Rocks, only spoiled by the sight of several crocodiles in the water. Another nice memory is when we went to the very old Monkey Temple. The servants had brought a banquet for us all to enjoy.

We caught the train from Delhi to Bombay, at Bombay we learned that our journey back to England was to be on the HMS Navasa again. Even after 6 years there had been no improvement in conditions on the ship. It rolled itself across the Indian Ocean, we encountered storms as we sailed through the Red Sea, and it was with relief that we found a haven as we made our way slowly through the Suez Canal. We spent several days sight seeing in Alexandria and then sailed on through to the Mediterranean where we enjoyed glorious sunshine, blue skies and the sea like a mill pond. It was when we came out of the Straits of Gibraltar that the weather changed and from then on it was storms, with rain and cold winds. Because we were dressed in clothing suitable for India my brother and I sat on deck wrapped in blankets from our beds to try to keep warm. There was nowhere else during the day to shelter as our cabins were being cleaned by the staff. Because

My mother and her friends on an outing to Marble Rocks

Bullock and Cart. Painted by John Price

of the rough weather and the ship rolling and pitching, the toilets were in great demand by the passengers so we chose to stay on deck and face the wind and rain until we docked at Southampton.

I remember one sad part of our journey home. We were all summoned on deck to attend the funeral service of a young soldier who had died on the ship. We were told that the sharks in the sea always follow the ship, they sensed that someone was dead, and knew that the burial would be for the body to be put in the sea.

The body of the dead soldier was wrapped in the Union Jack, laid on a board, as the music played and we sang hymns the board was lifted up to the rails and the body slid into the sea. What ever happened after I did not wait to see.

BACK TO BLIGHTY

Southampton docks was our first view of England. We disembarked from the ship, hoping that when we waved goodbye to the ship it would be for the last time. We made our way to the nearest restaurant for a hot cup of tea. We were a most unusual crowd of people dressed in such unsuitable clothes in the middle of winter. It has always been a surprise to me, and I am sure to others, for the Army authorities to regularly send home families from India, during the hottest part of the year to the coldest part of the year in Great Britain. It certainly was a shock to us all to feel and see ice and snow for the first time.

Our father had gone to get us a taxi, we were travelling to my mother's relations in Crowborough, Kent. I fell asleep and did not wake up until we arrived at my aunt and uncles house. Later I found out that they were my great great grandfather and great great grandmother. Why it was kept a secret I will never know. They greeted us kindly, but it was the first time I had seen white haired old people, and I was very shy. I could not believe my eyes when I saw the blazing fire in their lounge. The last time I had seen fire was when our house was hit by lightening, and saw the terrible damage it had done. The meal we were offered was so different from what we were accustomed to eating in India, my mother said it would be so rude to refuse to eat it.

We stayed with them for a week, and I met my auntie Flossie and her daughters, then we had to travel to London to meet my father's relations. I can only remember a stream of relations coming and going, and all remarked how sunburnt my brother and I were, and what a wonderful experience we were lucky to have had, spending six years in India when they had never experienced any sort of ship journey.

My father had been told that we would all be going to Cornwall where he would be stationed. He thought the family would be living in Torpoint.

It was December, and I saw for the first time the white covered English country side as we travelled by train. My impression of this cold miserable country was not at all favourable. I could not believe my eyes when we eventually arrived in London. Where did all the people come from, and where ever did they go. I was amazed at the made up roads going in all directions, and houses everywhere. I had never seen brightly lit shops, or even street lights before. Everywhere seemed crammed with cars and buses, I

Torpoint Ferry

wondered how did the people exist in such chaos. We had visited relations in London for a short while and bought winter clothes before we travelled to Devon where my father would be stationed in the Barracks for a few years. Our home was in Torpoint, Cornwall so we had to get on the ferry in Devonport to cross the River Tamar to Torpoint, our new home was in Mount Edgecombe Terrace. It took us months to settle in to such a different environment. We had been so young when we left England. Both my brother and I were so sun burnt that we looked like foreigners, also we spoke with a definite Indian dialect, when mother was not listening we put on a sing song speech, well known in 2007 but never heard in 1937.

My brother and I had a few of days freedom and then my father said it was time we went to school, he said it was somewhere in Torpoint and we should go along on our own and sign in. This casual information was a shock to us, we had forgotten school and the necessity to remember it had been pushed right to the back of our minds.

Next morning my mother came to the front door and pointed to the West and told us school was in that direction and I was to follow my brother. In fact it was nearly a mile and the only way we recognized the building was a school was because it was surrounded by a playground. There was not a soul in sight. My brother walked into the nearest building with me trailing behind. We were still in our Indian clothes. In the classroom I could only see boys, and the master took one look at me and said, "what have we here?" My brother Peter said we have come to school. The head master said you can stay by all means but your sister must go to the girls school next door. That was my introduction to Torpoint school which stayed with me until we moved again. The children always treated me as the funny girl from India, who went into the boys school.

Peter enjoyed the same attention, we were certainly the odd couple. We were given sweets to speak Hindustani and as there were no dentists in India, as soon as we had been in Torpoint a week, my mother took me to the dentist to have a plate in my mouth to correct my projecting top teeth, that caused an added interest in my oddity.

We had a small garden at the front and back of our house, and as everyone was busy I was happy making a garden with a small rockery, but I needed more earth. As there was a huge field out the back I got a bucket and spade and when I was busy loading it with earth I was petrified when a huge man stood beside me and said, "What are you doing stealing that earth". I dropped everything and ran into the house thinking this must be one of the bad men that stole children away. I was hiding in my bedroom when there was a knock on the front door. My mother answered it, and I heard the man say, "I am sorry I must have frightened your daughter who was busy gardening at the back." My mother called me and explained this was a policeman and not a man to be frightened of, if ever I needed help this was the man I could talk to. I had never seen a policeman before, and I wondered how would I know one when and if I saw one again.

We were liking our stay in Torpoint, especially in the summer, in the winter we hibernated on the coldest days. We had a stream of relatives coming and going, taking advantage of a holiday in Cornwall. Again everyone remarked on how sunburnt my brother and I were, they thought we had been so lucky to spend six years in India, these were people who had never experienced any sort of ship journey in those early days, rather different from this day and age.

Our address being 25 Mount Edgecombe Terrace, Torpoint, it was not surprising we had a magnificent view from our lounge windows. We could see the Plymouth Hoe. The saying goes if you could see Plymouth Hoe it meant it was going to rain, if you could not see Plymouth Hoe it meant it was raining. We could watch the different Warships arriving as they made their way up the Tamar to Plymouth docks.

Everyday my dad had to travel to work to Devonport by Torpoint Ferry. We were always amused at the number of people that were late catching the Ferry, the men would even jump into the water rather than wait for the next Ferry to arrive.

When Plymouth Navy Week was celebrated, my brother and I were allowed to go on our own. I was a little nervous going alone with my brother knowing how unkind he could be, but my father had warned him to look after me so he would take notice of his orders. I was wrong. We started off quite well but suddenly I did not know if he was on the Ferry or not, because he was hiding.

We caught the bus from Devonport into Plymouth, and arrived at the Dockyard gates. The guards were surprised to see us without our parents, but Peter told them we had our parents permission. Peter always ran ahead so I had to run to keep up. I was not happy with him but the worst time was when we went on a huge ship, he left me to go to the toilet on the docks. I followed him down the gangway and saw him go into the Mens toilets. I waited and waited and started to get very worried.

Two sailors were watching us from the ship, after an hour they came down to talk to me. They asked where my brother had gone, I told them he was in the toilets so they went to look. When they came out they told me he was not there, and I should go home. They asked me where I lived. I told them that I lived in Torpoint, which was two buses away and I did not have any money to catch a bus, my brother had all the money. The sailor was just about to give me money when my brother arrived. The sailor hit him hard across his head, and asked him for our address so he could write to my father for leaving me outside a Mens toilet for over an hour.

Peter was a little frightened of them and promised he

would take me home if I did not tell my mother about him leaving me. I agreed knowing Peter so that I could get home. Then when we arrived in Torpoint I foolishly said I would tell my mother. Peter laughed and said I did not give them our right address. I could never get my own back with Peter.

There was no comparison with our school in Torpoint and the school we went to in Jabalpur, India which was very basic. In this new school I spent most of my time in class wondering whatever the teacher was talking about. The only lesson I enjoyed was Geography, I excelled in that subject, our travels had taken us to countries that the other pupils had not even heard about.

Life was so different for us in Torpoint, England, we were older and so it took us a longer time to adjust. The area around our home in the barracks in Jabalpur was the playground for my brother and me. There were no restrictions such as dangerous roads to cross, we knew the area so well so we never got lost. Only when we went into the jungle many miles from the barracks to see the wild animals did we get lost. We spent a lot of time in the back bazaar especially when there was a religious ceremony, and the elephants were decorated in paint and coloured materials. It was very interesting to watch and we were given all sorts of highly coloured sweets by the Indians and invited to join in the celebration of the Ransaamy.

The animal and bird population in India was so different from Torpoint. There were no Monkeys in the trees and we did not have to worry about the snakes on the ground.

I had always been fascinated with the variety of brightly coloured birds, and the kites known for their scavenging whenever food was about. I even miss the cheeky monkeys who were everywhere, they came down from the trees when they saw an opportunity to steal anything they could eat. Peter was always busy with his air rifle and catapult. I was more than pleased when he missed his target. These were fond memories from the past. But now I had to adjust to a completely different life in Torpoint, Cornwall.

Before we were due to return to England my mother lectured us, we would never be allowed to wander alone, we must always stay together and never stray on our own, as there were nasty and dangerous men in England who would steal us away. With this dire warning no wonder I had not looked forward with pleasure to a place where bad men were on the prowl.

From the day we docked at Southampton docks, and all our journeys to visit relations, then on the long journey to Torpoint I held tightly to my mother's hand whenever we were taken out.

We had settled into our life in Torpoint, we all enjoyed walking so found our way to Whitsands, a beautiful sandy beach that was only five miles from our house so we went there often through the summer.

Then my father was ordered to go to Exeter, Devon, and life changed again. This time we lived in an annex to the main huge old building called the Priory, The Friars, this had been a Priory taken over many years ago by the Army. The rest of the building was the Army offices. On the grounds at the rear was the hall where Army exercises took place. The shooting range at the rear of the hall was a great attraction to my brother, who collected pistols and guns from his own collection and used them there when the hall was supposed to be locked and barred.

The whole area of the Priory had a ten foot wall surrounding it and with so much ground we were pleased that at last we could keep a dog. I would have taken time to choose a pedigree dog, but my father brought home from the local pet shop a black and white mongrel, we named her Pat. No one in the family knew anything about injections for Hard Pad and Distemper so it was not surprising that Pat died of Distemper at the age of two.

The Priory consisted of buildings which were built in

the early 1860's. All our relations chose to visit us as we had so many bedrooms. This was not a happy situation as before long our home became a hotel. As to be expected when Aunts, Uncles and cousins descended on us at all times. The worse time was when one Aunt and cousin stayed for a month, and when she left, she decided that she could not cope with her teenage son anymore, so she left him with my father (his Uncle) to bring him into line. This took more effort than my father was willing to put into the change. The day my cousin became fourteen he was told to pack his suitcase, and my father took him to join the Army. My father said to us as he left the house with a shocked nephew (the Army will make a man out of him).

It was not long before my father's mother (my grand-mother), who was seventy but healthy, came to live with us. A week after she arrived, her grandson (my cousin) who had been put in the Army arrived on leave. One day a policeman was knocking at our front door, my grandmother went to answer the door. The policeman asked her does Colonel Stone live here. My grandmother told him yes he does but is not at home at the moment. Then he asked her do you have a young soldier, his nephew staying here? My grandmother said yes he was here. The policeman answered, "we understand that he has left the barracks to attend his grandmother's funeral". Just then my father arrived, and after a word with the policeman my cousin was brought out looking very nervous. I heard no more but my cousin was not at dinner that night.

There was a huge oak tree in front of the Priory car park. Peter decided he was going to build a tree house above the ten foot wall he brought wood and roofing and was soon busy with hammer and nails. Everything went well until my father came home after being away for a fortnight and was undressing in his bedroom, he looked out of his bedroom window and saw us seated in our tree house just two foot away from his bedroom. The tree house was immediately torn down and we were in disgrace.

Peter then decided he was going to use the attic to fix up a telephone connection from one attic to another. This was very successful until he walked into a part of the attic that was over the main entrance hall to the office building, where the officers and visitors entered on Special Army occasions. Peter should have walked carefully on the cross beams, but instead walked and fell through the ceiling of the sixteen foot high hall, was only saved from serious injury because he had sense enough to save himself by holding onto the crossbeams with both arms.

My father came out of his office when he heard the noise of the plaster falling onto the floor, he looked up to see my brother's legs dangling from the high ceiling and yelling for help.

I was very lucky to have passed the entrance exam and been accepted into Bishop Blackall Grammar School for girls. Peter had missed so much schooling with our moves every few years that he did not pass and had to go to a council school, this did not bother him at all as he knew that when he reached the age of 14 years old he would be in the Army, which was his life long ambition.

I had to walk every day to school across the grounds of Exeter Cathedral, on through the town and by the beautiful garden of Northern Hay, pass Exeter prison to the school. A most interesting walk, lovely in the summer, but not so pleasant in the winter. As a soldier's daughter I saw the winter through, enjoyed the summer, and had a good idea that by the next winter we would be on the move again.

It was not surprising when we were told that our next move was to be Wanstead Park London. This time my parents decided to buy a private house. But my father was stationed at Stratford Barrack being able to travel home every day. I had left school and hoped to choose work in a hairdresser's shop, or work in a dress shop, but I had

The Priory the Friars
Exeter

George Ernest on leave
Wansted Park

no choice, my father decided to send me to Pitmans College, Forest Gate, London, in order to learn shorthand and typing and other accomplishments for office work. At this time it was 1937 and I was 14 years old and Peter was 15. A few days after arrival at Wanstead Park, my father took my brother, Peter to join the Army as a Boy Soldier, at Hillsea Barracks, Portsmouth to be in the Royal Army Ordinance Corp.

My father had risen in the ranks and was also an officer, so it seemed that we might be settled for a while in Wanstead Park. It was an ideal place to own dogs, there were miles and miles of country walks, and the park itself was a haven of wild life, woods and lakes. We bought a wire fox terrier and named him Nicki.

Our family life seemed settled, again I was proved to be wrong. There was talk and rumours about appending war with Germany and my father was away more often, even his yearly manoeuvres were cancelled, we knew it was serious when he packed his bags and told us he was going to be stationed up north, he gave us no address we were told nothing else, he would be writing. As we lived away from the Barracks everything that we heard was second hand, rumours about the pending war were talked about everywhere. We got a nasty surprise from his first letter that we were definitely at war with Germany.

A week later coming home from College I was very surprised to see the busy activity on the Wanstead Flats. A whole area was being cordoned off with a ten foot barb wire fence, huts were being built and soldiers were busy everywhere. I was told it was to be a concentration camp at first then it was to be a German prisoner of war camp.

We lived only a few miles from Woolwich docks and would be right in the centre of trouble. In the fields behind our house there was a search light battallion, and when the planes came over London, before the barrage balloons were used the planes dived and shot out the search lights

My Dads manouvers just before the war

Peter in Hillsea Barracks, Boy Sargeant

which peppered the roof of our house with shrapnel. Daily we watched tanks and bren gun carriers in their hundreds passing through the main road to the Woolwich docks.

My mother and I were issued with ration books, and clothes coupons. I cannot remember what our ration was for the week, but I know that I was very hungry, food and clothes seemed to disappear from the shops. The air raid warnings were sounded regularly but the German planes did not come to our part of the country at the beginning, in fact hardly anyone took notice, as we imagined it was a false alarm. A few days later the air raid sirens went off one evening. The anti aircraft guns on Wanstead Flats went on throughout the night, we saw flames rising high in the sky and guessed this was an air attack on Woolwich Docks. We heard the damage to houses and factories and deaths were so bad that the docks would be out of commission for months. My mother was advised I should be evacuated to a safer place. The bombs were dropped nightly. It became so dangerous to live in that area.

I had a few friends but all had been evacuated and we had lost touch. Once or twice I went to the cinema but most of my time I was taking the dog for a walk in the Park. He loved it, I took sandwiches to share.

Quite often a Buzz bomb went over, he let me know long before it arrived, and jumped on the hill-lock of earth from the hundreds of Dugouts to bark at the Buzz bomb that went over, he might have come into the shelter with me but had to bark his annoyance.

Next day I was shopping for our rations, and a soldier came to knock on our door from the Searchlight unit in the field behind our house.

He spoke to my mother, that he had seen me walking the dog and he hoped we could get married before he was sent overseas.

Guessing my mothers answer I was not surprised that

I never saw him again.

He and several others used to wave to me, they still continued, but my mothers answer must have changed his mind about his wish to have her as his Mother-in -Law.

LEAVING HOME AT FIFTEEN

I left Pitmans College and I was given a job with the Board of Education in Holborn Kingsway as a shorthand typist. I had to travel by train to London every day and often we would have to lay on the floor as the German planes came down low to machine gun the trains. The shorthand typist pool was on the thirteenth floor of the building and every time the air raid warning went off we all had to rush down the stairs as the lift was not used in case we were hit. It soon became very difficult for us having to sit in the basement unable to do any work for hours. Then we heard that the Board of Education was evacuating its staff and offices from Holborn Kingsway to Bournemouth and I was advised to go with them. I was now 15 years old and I was going to live away from my mother for the first time.

The different government offices that had been evacuated down there from London were blamed by the residents for the attack as there had been no sign of the war before we came. Information must have been passed around that spies had been busy giving away the information that government offices were now in Bournemouth, The Board of Education, the Board of Trade, Shell Mex.

We were told to make our way to our first billet at Westbourne Park Road. The landlady told us she had only two bedrooms but had put extra beds in them, so the girls must share beds as there was little room for more. I had never shared a bed with anyone, so I asked if I could have a bed for myself alone. The landlady said she could only offer me a bed in the attic.

Life was very quiet and pleasant for two days, we were

A picture of me stood outside Durley Dene Hotel in Bournemouth

delighted to be so near the sea with such a beautiful view from our house. Next morning we went to the Durley Dene Hotel that had been converted into offices for the Board of Education office staff.

The next night I was woken up by a frightening explosion, falling plaster and glass, and as the lights went out I could only see light from the night stars and the moon above me. I could hear the girls downstairs, shouting and crying. I looked for the stairs to escape and they were not there. So the best thing to do was to get dressed and wait for someone to rescue me. This was in the middle of the night and I saw a ladder being put up to the attic window. I heard a man's voice telling me that there was no window glass, so could I get to the window to climb down. The only thought that I had in my mind was “thank goodness I got dressed.” Later I heard that the house opposite was completely demolished and our house was badly damaged. The other six girls were able to walk out of the house, as their bedrooms were on the first floor. But as I had been given a bedroom in the attic, when part of the roof was blown off, the attic stairs were damaged so I could not get to the stairs. While waiting I decided to pack my clothes in my case and wait.

Our work offices at Durley Dene Hotel were not far from our billets. The shorthand typists were allocated a huge beautifully decorated dance hall to work in. We could look out of the large windows and see the sea. We tried not to remember that not all that too far away was France and Germany. So many rumours were spread around at that time, many of the staff had husbands and boyfriends fighting across that beautiful sea view. The evacuation of Dunkirk and the fact that at any time we could be bombed or invaded was included in all our conversation. The cliffs were out of bounds to civilians, we guessed that they had been set with land mines. In fact when we took our regular walks along the cliffs we took photos of each other with the sea in the background. One day the soldiers that lived on the sands and guarded the cliffs next to the Durley Chines told us that we were on dangerous grounds and confiscated our camera and warned us not to take any more photos of that part of the cliff. We could see there were buildings of all sorts on the sands, and we should have realized that we were trespassing on Army grounds, the steel girders sticking up in the sea, and the barbed wire fences should have given us a clue.

A week later the photos from the camera we had taken were sent to our office supervisor, with a letter in her hand we all thought she had received a complaint about us trespassing on Army property, and we were in trouble. Instead it was an invitation asking her if she would arrange for several of her staff to come to an evening entertainment, and dance with the injured Airmen and Soldiers in the Hospital on the beach. They would send a lorry for us to be collected and returned.

She had agreed that several of us accepted the invitation and would be pleased to come. We looked forward to the dance. We were welcomed by a doctor, who warned us that many of the patients were badly disfigured, several had lost an arm, and there were many in wheelchairs. He asked us if we would circulate and talk to those who could not dance.

This was the first time that we had seen that side of the ravages of war. We had seen houses demolished, many of us had been bombed out in London, and we had heard about terrible atrocities but here we were face to face with the real tragedies of war.

I was asked if I would dance with an Airman with part of his face burnt, and disfigured down his neck. I am tall and his poor face was right next to mine. We had been told not to mention anything about the war, and not to ask questions about their injuries, just to act normally. On the way home from the dance no one could speak, we were all so terribly shocked and upset. We had treated the war as a difficult situation that we had to put up with but it was far away and it did not affect us. We joked about when the Germans would be invading, but the evening spent with those poor crippled and injured men brought us closer to the reality of war. We were invited again the following week, but my supervisor saw how the evening had affected me, she told me she had chosen an older woman to take my place. I was ashamed to be pleased.

We were all expected to take our turn at fire watching Durley Dene offices throughout the night. Then it was my turn to be on the roof, I was given a steel helmet, Wellington boots (two sizes too large), surplus stock Army overalls, and trousers.

Firewatching in Bournemouth 1939

If incendiary bombs were dropped on the roof of the building, I had a shovel, bucket of sand and another bucket filled with water. The two men on watch with me said they had to stay downstairs and visit all the buildings and offices every hour. I wondered how they arranged it that they were downstairs in the warmth and I was on the roof in the cold. I had noticed two beds with blankets that had been used when I left in the morning.

We learnt later that it was one of the land mines dropped on the house opposite, and the blast damaged so many houses in the vicinity. We were all told to collect our belongings and take them to the offices at Durley Dene Hotel.

We were split into smaller groups and sent to a different billet on Poole Road. The Board of Education had made a very important mistake by putting all the Clerical Officers in our house, the Accountants in another, and part of the Shorthand Typist and Typist in a house on their own. When the bombs dropped on the different houses, whole departments were decimated. Just seven of us were sent to Poole

Road, the others were sent nearer the town of Poole.

We were crammed into a smaller house, it was a three storey building above a sweet shop. The owner was so pleased to have us there, each month when his ration of sweets arrived, we bought the whole lot, and he did not need to open his shop at all.

There was just one communal bathroom, lavatory, and sink provided for us to share. The morning queueing was chaos as we all scrambled to get ready for work. The cry for entry to the bathroom, was followed by, "Let me in I won't look".

Living under those conditions made me decide to try to join the ATTS, WAFF, or the Womans Land Army. The houses to apply to join were on the outskirts of Bournemouth.

I went to the first house which housed the Air Force, they took one look at me and asked if I was running away from home. The next house was the Army, I was given a form to fill in. I decided it would be more successful if I put my age a year older than sixteen. The lady behind the counter asked me if I had my parents permission. I told them that my father was a Colonel in the Army and he would keep his eye on me. She said to me, "If he is a Colonel he would be too busy winning the war, and much too busy to keep his eye on a fifteen year old girl".

I was getting very disappointed with the reception I was getting, so I tried the next house expecting to get the same response. It was a real pleasure to be greeted so nicely by the Womans Land Army receptionist. I filled in the form, they did not ask my age, they told me I would be called for duty at Sparsholt Training College near Winchester in 2 weeks.

My father had heard from my brother that I was thinking of leaving the Board of Education and join the ATTS. He immediately said he would arrange for me to join him in the North, this way he would be able to keep his eye on my activities. I did try to join the ATTS but they did not accept me as I was too young, but the Womens Land Army were so keen to get girls to work on the land they did not ask me my age. I had heard that there were only Greyhound kennels given permission to have help during the war, so I applied. My letter must have gone astray because I was sent to a chicken and pig farm.

Although I lived in a billet with several women, it was a very lonely life, as I was so much younger than all of them. Many were married but their husbands were away fighting, others had men friends. I was very pleased to receive a letter from my father telling me he was sending me the rail fare for me to spend a week with him up North. His barracks were in a town near Newcastle Upon Tyne, but I would not be allowed to stay with him, a friend would be pleased to be my companion for the week. He said it would be wise not to tell my mother as she was unable to travel up North and leave the bomb damaged house. I had not seen my father for over a year, so I was pleased that he said he would pick me up at the station and take me to his friend's house.

It was a long journey from Bournemouth to Newcastle Upon Tyne. It was a huge station I was so relieved to see my father waiting for me, he introduced me to a lady who was standing with him only as Pauline, who was to be my companion for the week. I would be staying with her as she owned a large Hotel. As the week went by my father came everyday to the Hotel, and sometimes stayed the night.

It suddenly dawned on me that Pauline was the reason he never had time to go home to my mother. He had given my mother so many excuses that he was so busy with the pending war, and he had to go on many training sessions with his men. In fact it struck me that I was right in the middle of my father cheating on my mother. I had to stay the rest of the week in Pauline's home, they must have been quite sure that I was innocent of the situation as I was only fifteen. I was hiding my feelings but could not wait to leave them. When we got to the station, Newcastle Upon Tyne, over fifteen miles from their home, I realized that I had left my train ticket on the table beside my bed, there was no time to go back so my father had to purchase another ticket for me to get back to Bournemouth. He was livid.

When I got back to Bournemouth I received a letter from my mother, she had no idea I had been staying with my father. She said that my father had asked her to cash in her pensions and investments and send him the cash. He was a colonel in the Army, I had seen the rich way he lived, he had a beautiful new car, and he seemed to spend money with no bother about the future. I was in a horrible situation. No wonder he had asked me not to tell my mother I was staying up North with him. Now I knew why.

It was quite obvious that Peter, having stayed with them several times knew the situation, and had not told me or my mother. If I had known I certainly would not have gone to stay with them. I had to tell my mother the true situation, and also advise her not to send my father any money. I wondered if she would believe me that I was innocent of his double life.

My mother wrote to me a nice letter asking me when I was coming home, so when I had a weekend off I went to Wanstead Park.

Later during the War my father was invalided out the Army, so he and Pauline sold the Hotel, and bought a beautiful Shooting Lodge called Kirby Misperton, and also a Hotel in Brotherton. My father was not well so they decided to sell both properties and buy a Hotel in Ibiza. There my father lived a short while until he passed away, I had been told by my brother.

Back at Sparsholt Training College I was instructed to

Kirby Misperton Hall

go to a barn and get the chickens ready for market. That did not worry my unduly, but what did worry me was, I was to kill the chickens, pluck them, clean them out and then they would be ready for market. I was shown how to kill them, but I was not told to hold the wings and legs very tightly for a while as their reflexes would keep them flying about the room, blood was everywhere.

After all my training was finished I was sent to another huge chicken farm on the Hampshire Downs. I was billeted in a house two miles from the farm so I had to buy myself a bicycle which made a journey through the village lanes to the farm difficult in the winter. One day which was particularly icy, my bicycle slipped from under me and I nearly went under an Army lorry, thank goodness it had very good brakes. The soldiers jumped out to see if I was alright. It was no ones fault. That is how I met my future husband George Collis, he was in charge of the lorry and taking the men back to the Barracks. They drove me up to the farm with my bike which was not badly damaged. I had fallen heavily on my arm which was very painful. The owner of the farm drove me back to my billet.

I went back to work the following week, with my arm in a sling. One early morning I went to collect eggs from the hen houses. This farm was right in the lonely part of the Hampshire Downs, I had collected half a basket full of eggs and I opened the door of the next chicken house and came face to face with a German pilot, I assumed he had come down by parachute the night before. He was busy eating the raw eggs from the nest. Very shocked I can only remember saying, “Oh Hello” and turned and ran as fast as I could with my basket of eggs, back to the farm offices. They called the police and before long a lorry arrived from the Army camp to collect their prisoner.

One morning I arrived at the chicken farm to be told that the Vet had been and found fowl pest in many of the hens and cockerels, so all the staff would have to clean up and inject all the chickens on the farm. Our job was to clean out the muck, like cheese, in the chickens’ mouth, so that they could breath, and then inject them in their legs. This took all the staff the whole week. None were killed and none died. We were not given any protection like gloves nor a mask, and no one got ill. I wondered why the fowl pest outbreak in England last year was not treated the same way. Why were so many chickens killed and burnt?.

The arm I had fallen on became very painful so I went to the doctor who told me that I had broken a bone, so I had to have the arm in plaster and carried it in a sling. I was unable to do my job properly, it was then I was invalided out of the Land Army, so I went home to Wanstead Park.

My mother was working regularly at the post office. My father was now a full Colonel and still stationed in the North. The War seemed never ending. A friend had a litter of Sealyham Terrier puppies so I decided to buy one. I named him Brett Haggis. He was a lively pup, not fright-

Brett Haggis our Sealyham Terrier

ened of anything. He barked at the planes as they went over, ignored the guns and bombs that landed nearby.

One terrible night another house in our road was badly damaged, our front door was blown up the passageway, Brett took the opportunity to dash out into the road and started fighting with another dog who had gained his freedom the same way. With all the noise, police cars, ambulances and fire engines it was the last straw for the neighbours to contend with two fighting dogs. The police tried to catch him, but he slunk away and returned home later as if nothing had happened. We found him scratching away in his bed where all the glass from the broken windows had fallen.

My mother had to leave for work every day, so I was in charge of the shopping for food, and cleaning the house. Not that there was much I could do for both. The shopping chore was to stand in a queue for our tiny rations for about an hour. Sometimes I was lucky enough to arrive just at the same time as the food lorry. Our home was damaged so badly and had not been repaired at all. The windows had been covered in wood and black paper. Struts were still up in our lounge. When the air raid warning sounded the only thing I could do was to take the dog down the cellar and read a book.

We were offered a garden air raid shelter, but my mother and I had no desire to go out in the dark every night.

We moved into the cellar to live for several days until our front door was replaced, the windows were boarded up and struts were put into place to hold the rest of the sitting room ceiling up. My mother received a letter from Auntie Vincent (my great grandmother who was 97 and now a widow) she told my mother that life in Folkestone was so dangerous now so could she come to stay with us at Wanstead Park. My mother said of course she could come but did she realize that the house was damaged and we were living in the cellar. We did not hear anything from her, but four days later she arrived driven by her grandson. For two nights running we had no bombers, there was a lull in all Army activities. Auntie Vincent told us that she was very pleased she came as life was so much easier and not so stressful in our house. She could not have taken a lot of notice of the windows boarded up, the new front door had arrived, but we still had the struts holding up the ceiling in the sitting room. When she came down to the cellar for her meals, she used to say, “haven’t you made it nice and cozy down here”.

One day later I was on my way home from shopping, when the siren went, so I made my way into the air raid shelter on the Flats that had been built for such an emergency. It was a shelter built with an entrance one end, and about a quarter of a mile further was the exit. I could hear the anti aircraft guns were busy so I decided to walk all the way underground to the exit so that I would be closer to home when the all clear went. Some people in the shelter as I passed by had brought blankets to settle down to sleep expecting an all night bombing. I had just arrived at the exit when there was a terrific explosion, a bomb had been dropped at the entrance and people were killed. I ran out of the shelter as fast as I could and met my mother who had come to look for me, she had hear the bombs dropping and as I was very late she was worried.

George Collis had gone back to France I had received one letter from him, telling me that he was due a leave soon. It was not long before the employment authorities checked me, I was just seventeen and had left the Land Army, I should have gone straight into another important job.

They sent me to The Northern Outfall factory it meant I would have two journeys by bus, and then a mile walk along the banks of the river Thames very near Woolwich Docks. A frightening journey in peace time, and unbearable in war time. I was so pleased when George Collis came home on a weekend leave, just in time to go to the Authorities to tell them I was not trying to get out of working, but I was a qualified shorthand typist and should be used as such. I was not at the meeting but they must have been impressed by him as they gave me a shorthand typist job at Plesseys in Ilford only a short bus ride for me from Wanstead Park. Plesseys were making bombs and tanks in the factory. It was not surprising that at my first day at work the German planes machine gunned the offices, and we all had to lay flat on the ground with arms over our head because of the flying glass. Two weeks later I was very pleased to see the Air Force putting up the Barrage Balloons to stop the planes from flying low.

George came on leave as we had planned to go to church to meet the Vicar to have our wedding banns called. I had worked late several evenings but this was an important engagement. The office supervisor Mr. MacMurdie said that I had to work that evening or he would send me down the tunnel to work on the hardest machine they had down there. Plesseys had taken over the built underground train stations at Gants Hill onwards. All their secret machines were down there, it was a miserable place for the workers but they made the best of it because at least it was safe. To be sent down the Tunnel to work for the office staff, was the boss's favourite threat to anyone who dared to oppose him.

He was a real bully, and I thought it best to give in. When my husband to-be heard that I had to stay to work and could not keep our appointment that evening, he said he would have a word with Mr MacMurdie. I do not know what was said, but we went to the meeting with the Vicar as planned.

I tried everyday to take Brett to the park. One day I noticed a small plane coming over the tree tops. It could not be an enemy bomber as the air raid warning had not gone off, so I continued with my walk. Suddenly the engine cut out, and it came down in a big circle, the flames from the back of the plane had stopped and as it came lower I grabbed Brett and dived for shelter in one of the dugouts. There was an almighty explosion as it landed near the church on the hill. I saw the church disappear, rubble flew everywhere it was a terrible sight. Brett stood on top of the earth from the dugout and barked his annoyance as his daily walk had been interrupted. I realized that hundreds more were to follow.

A relation had to be evacuated and could not take her Scottish Terrier, Robert Burns McKenzie Campbell, so we offered to board him for a short while, rather than let him be put to sleep. Robert did not take to Brett, and Brett certainly did not take to Robert. We had our job cut out trying to keep them apart. Every night when we made arrangements to retire, Robert would get under the table and no amount of calling, baiting and threatening would make him come out. So we decided we would fool him and hours before we would be going to bed we had to grab him by the scuff of his neck and take him out to the kennels. He soon caught on to this and went under the table earlier and earlier. My mother was passing the table not knowing that he had retreated for the night, as she stood there he jumped out and bit her through her shoe. This was enough suffering for my parent to bear, so Robert Burns McKenzie Campbell was taken to the Vet.

George Collis and I were married in St. Gabriel's Church Wanstead Park in 1941. A year later our daughter Carol was born, because of the bombing situation the doctor took me to Wanstead Nursing Home three days before Carol was born.

During those three days I wondered wether it would have been safer at home, most of the time we lived down the cellar, where beds had been quickly arranged for the four pregnant expecting mothers. George came home to see his newly born daughter but then had to return to Germany. The sleeping arrangements at home were difficult as repairs to the house had never taken place. The arrangement was that my mother slept on the couch, and I made the bed for Carol and myself on the floor behind two large chairs, Auntie Vincent had the small back bedroom where she felt comfortable on her own.

The Germans were now sending Buzz Bombs in their hundreds to our country, there was no point in sounding the air raid warning as they came over throughout the day and night. I was advised by the authorities to take my daughter Carol away from what was called Buzz Bomb Alley. My sister in law, Lily had already gone to Scotland with her relations so I decided to travel to Scotland where we ought be safe. It may not have been a good decision to stay with all my in-laws in our situation but I had no choice. Now Carol and I were living with my mother in-law in the same house in Barrhead, Scotland with all her

Cyril George Collis

friends, her daughter Lily and her daughter Rose, and Carol was spoiled badly.

Life was so difficult I decided to return back to Wanstead Park. I made my way from Barrhead, Scotland by bus, with Carol, pushchair and large suitcase so many kind people helped me on the bus and off again at Glasgow station. There were soldiers everywhere offering me help. I found my way to the rail carriage. I had Carol on my lap and a soldier put my large suitcase on the rack above my head. The train started off with a huge jerk and the case dropped off on my head, it knocked me out. There was a doctor on the train, and when I came too he was attend-

Joyce and Carol in Scotland

ing to my bruised head, and the four soldiers in the compartment were looking after Carol. I was so pleased when that journey ended. When I got home I found out that my Auntie Vincent had gone back to Folkstone, she thought that it was too dangerous at Wanstead Park, little did she know that the Germans had another secret weapon to send over after the Buzz Bomb had finished and they would land first in Folkstone.

I had one enjoyable day when I was delighted to hear that there was a sale of cot blankets in the local market, so off I went. I had not had such an enjoyable fun day for years. The Cot blankets were imported from abroad and were brightly coloured greens, blues, browns and patterned. My clothing coupons had run out and I had to beg coupons from relations, I looked for two blankets of the same colour, one for the front of my dress that I intended to make and the same colour for the back. Other buyers were in the queue scrambling to get matching pairs, it was great fun.

I was not surprised to see so many women at the sale, as cot blankets did not need coupons and were not rationed. It was obvious they had been sent for mothers with babies. They did not care what colour they had. We were told that the Americans had shipped them over as there was space in one of their cargo ships that were full of tinned goods for us starving Britains. We appreciated the food but it was also nice for us to improve our wardrobe of shabby old fashion clothes. The next time we went to the market there were

The Family Collis in Wellyn

Carol and Jean

Me, Jean and the dog walking in Wanstead Park

piles of curtain material for sale, no doubt from the same source. So many girls and women were in uniforms, but it was a real change to have a new dress or skirt, even if it was made of cot blanket or curtain material.

No sooner did we get used to the Buzz Bombs coming over regularly everyone stopped to watch as we heard the unmistakable motorbike noise as they went overhead. Then the Germans decided that they would use another secret weapon the Rockets fired from the French coast and aimed anywhere in the South of England. There was no warning the rockets hit the ground, or house, or factory, and then exploded, at least we did get a warning from the Buzz Bombs we could watch them fly overhead and it was impossible not to be relieved when the machine continued flying further out of sight. There was nothing we could do when the engine stopped in the Buzz Bomb but there was time to dash for the shelter. There was not time to escape the rockets, that is why so many people were killed.

My second daughter Jean was born over two years later at my mother's house at Wanstead Park. My husband was away in Germany and my mother suggested to me that I move to Welling, Kent with my two daughters as she did not want her home made into a nursery.

My husband George was still in Germany although the War was over, I did not know when he would be returning, so I moved furniture, cots and bed to Welling, Kent to await his return. It was a very small house and my mother in-law and father in-law lived upstairs while I and the two children had two rooms downstairs. I was not happy there but I had no choice. There was only one toilet which was in the garden out at the back of the house and any visitors, as well as those living upstairs, had to come through my living room to reach the toilet.

My mother-in-law loved the children as she was always asking for me to leave them with her and when I had been there for a year I heard that there was to be a Dog Show in Danson Park, Welling, Kent and as it was quite near to where we lived at that time I decided to go. Our family, like all other families had such a miserable time during and immediately after the war, so many restrictions, rations and very little pleasures, that any sort of entertainment was to be grabbed at and enjoyed.

MY LOVE AFFAIR WITH DOGS

NO one else in the family considered that a Dog Show was pleasure, so I left home early in the morning to make my way to Danson Park. It was a small Open Show, and two marquees had been erected to house the rings and the dogs.

I wandered around in a dream, in the marquees were benches for the dogs to rest in until their class was to be judged. I did not know a soul, but never for one minute did I feel in need of human company. I watched one class being judged, and it must have been beginners luck as I had picked out the same winners as did the judge. Then when the next class came into the ring and I also picked out the winners before the judge had placed them, I was very proud of myself. I cannot remember the breed, and I cannot remember the name of the judge. I had never read an educational dog book.

My attention was also taken up with the judge, he was very impressively dressed in a well cut suit, and a large colourful badge with the word JUDGE written on it. The applause that was given to him as he placed his winners was obviously why he had an air of satisfaction. He was truly a judge that loved dogs, and enjoyed every minute of his time in the centre of the ring. It would be times like that which would give untried but enthusiastic beginners their goals in life, and it was there and then that my ambition for the future was to be eventually a judge of dogs. It was a most improbable dream, we had little money, and I had two very young daughters. None of the rest of the family liked dogs, and my husband had made the rule one dog is enough in any home.

As the tents were being taken down, and the dogs were leaving the venue with their owners, mostly walking as there were very few cars used for pleasure travelling in those days, I also made my way home. I decided that it would be wisest to keep my ambition to myself, and revert to being a housewife and mother until an opportunity arose to buy a pedigree dog, learn about the breed and then train to be a judge. That was in 1955.

George was demobbed from the Army and decided to take a job in the Prison Service. He thought it was a safe job with regular income but he was very unhappy with that harsh environment and soon left. The girls were also unhappy living in a small house with our relations and we were more than pleased when he accepted a manager's position in a shop in Ashford, Kent. This meant he had to buy a house near the shop. We were so pleased with this home, a nice large garden in a lovely country area. Also importantly the house was not far from a school as both Carol and Jean had started to go to school. It was a very nice comfortable house. What made it so attractive was the fact that a bus which stopped outside took us to the seaside at Hythe.

Sadly we were there only for one year, when George came home to tell us he had been offered a position of manager of a shop in Baldock, in Hertfordshire and this meant we would be living above the shop in the middle of town. We were very upset, we hid our tears and started packing. We three simply had to accept it.

When we moved to Baldock, I was so pleased to be in amongst so many keen dog owners in the area so much so I soon was visiting dog shows and dog activities. I was so pleased to make friends in such a town and this area was full of dog people and dog activities. Some were committee members of the various canine societies, and it was not long before I was invited to join some of them and I agreed to be voted onto their committee. I was involved in so many dog activities that eventually I was on the committee of 13 societies, one that was my favourite was Hitchin and District Canine Society. In later years I became their Secretary. Being so active in dog activities I extended my interest in Obedience. I was approached with an invitation to join their Obedience Club. I intended to buy a Beagle and I knew it was a breed that definitely needed a lot of training. I had met many Beagle owners when I joined the Pack when we lived in Exeter.

They were merry little dogs and as we were to live in a flat not difficult to keep clean, as they would need very little grooming. I heard of a litter for sale, and a friend of mine also wanted to buy a Beagle dog. As I knew Mrs. Scott he went with me to see the litter, she brought the litter into the room in a plastic bath tub, they looked very nice and typically English breeding. I asked her which were the pets, and which were the potential show pups. She said, "the one you pick will be for show and will cost £30, the one your friend chooses will be just a pet and cost £15." I was most annoyed to be asked to pay for my own knowledge so refused to buy a pup, but I did point out to my friend to pick the lemon and white dog, which was in my opinion, an outstanding quality pup. He bought it for £15. Mrs Scott phoned me later to say that I could buy the Tri coloured bitch for £15, so I was very pleased to have Merry Maid Of Thunderdell, as a brood bitch.

A few weeks later I was very upset to learn Mr. Johns and his wife had parted, and while he was at work he had to leave the Beagle puppy dog shut up in a cupboard. I begged him to sell me the puppy and he agreed. With no further use for it he sold it to me for just £1. The dog's name was Kipper, and as he was sold as a pet Mrs. Scott had not registered him with the Kennel Club. Kipper made continual amorous advances to Merry Maid, and as I had

The first meeting of the Hitchin & District Canine Society

no facilities to keep them apart I let him go to the Cornevon Kennels owned by Mr. and Mrs. Gibson who were famous for their Beagles and Irish Setters.

Kipper's name was registered with the Kennel club as Keeper of Highbury and used very extensively at stud. I was sad to see him go as he was such a character but in the Cornevon's kennels his randy behaviour was legitimatized with visiting bitches.

There was an obedience Club in Hitchin, so I decided to take Merry to some sort of Obedience training, then I could perhaps get her attention in the show ring. After several open meetings we found that an Obedience school was a dire need for the dogs in the Hitchin area, I was voted in as Secretary and the Club was called The North Herts dog Training Club. Our first meeting took place in a small wooden hut in Letchworth. The floor was not safe, the cold air came in through the cracks in the walls, but we were proud of our Club, whenever I was free I brought Merry in to do some exercise, but as I had hoped to show her eventually I allowed her to take the position of stand instead of at the 'SIT'.

Although I continued to be Secretary my first love was the show world. I had to admit that Merry would do very little in Obedience and less in the show world. So I bought a Tri coloured dog from Mrs. Gibson, he was called Cornevons Warbler. I heard that there was a Beagle Meet, organized by Mr. Douglas Appleton of the Appeline kennels. Many of the Beagle owners took their dogs with them, it proved more fun to see the pet Beagles revert to their natural instinct and join in the hunt with enthusiasm. It was music to our ears to hear our dogs give tongue following the professionals. To see them streaking over the fields in hot pursuit of the hare. We followed on, suitably dressed, in warm coats and trousers and Wellington boots. The pack disappeared into the distance and I guessed somewhere amongst them was my dog Warbler. He had forgotten me, this was the life he had been bred for, and he was going to take advantage of. We trudged over the muddy field, this way, and that way, we were far from any close activities of the pack, only the Baying of the hounds in the distance, and the shouts of the 'Whips' could be heard. Hours went by and dusk was settling in when the straggling pack and the green coated leaders returned. I searched through the muddy pack for my dog, he was nowhere to be seen. I started getting worried, so asked if anyone had seen my Tri coloured dog. Douglas Appleton asked me to describe him, I pointed out a randy little specimen, covered in mud that was trying continually to mount all the bitches that came within his vicinity. "That is your dog, and don't ever bring him again". I grabbed Warbler and took him home, bathed and dried he looked very sleepy and settled down to rest, no doubt dreaming of his wonderful experience in the muddy fields of Ashwell, with all those friendly bitches.

At the early stage the beagles were being shown at dog shows in very small numbers, but there were many pack owners in outlying districts that worked their Beagles at weekends. There was a little animosity from the pack owners and the show people as there has been, and will be in most breeds that eventually find their way into the show ring.

In 1954 the show people were allocated 10 sets of Challenge Certificate for Beagles at Championship shows. The best winning Beagles in 1955 were Mrs. Clayton's Champion (Ch) Barvae Paigan, and Mr. Watson's Ch. Barvae Statute. The first Beagle to win Best In Show on the first day at Crufts was Ch. Derawuda Vixen sired by Mr. Watson's Barvae Statute.

Beagles had found their way to America long before, and as always with a breed sent to that country they had been slightly altered in head, shape and colour. I remember the first American import when Mrs. Thelma Gray and Mrs. Beck purchased him, a small 12½ inch Beagle called Am. Ch. Renoca's Best Showman. With the imports from America the winning Beagles were a lot smaller in size, the larger hounds had less chance to win against the compact glamorous smaller type. The American bloodlines were dominant, and we were to see a majority of more black blankets and richer Tan markings, with the white trim making the dogs very eye catching to the judges. Heads were a lot squarer, with deep leathers and dark eyes in the Tri coloured Beagles. The patchy markings of the English Lemon and White Beagles, the Lemon Pied and the hare pied quite often seen in the show ring winning before the advent of the American imports did not do so well against the Tri-coloured evenly marked hounds.

It was difficult for me to breed from my Beagles at that time, so I decided to buy in a puppy bitch when I heard that Mrs. Gibson had a litter out of her Blossom of Cornevon.

She was all I wished for in a Beagle, beautifully marked, super long leathers, excellent construction, sound in front and rear. We had a very successful show career together.

Bliss, her shortened name, won several Best of Breed awards (BOB), then at one Open show she was placed BOB, then she won the hound group and finally Best In Show (BIS). I decided to show her at Crufts under the World famous judge Judy De Casembroot. Her method of judging was very unusual, as she examined each bitch in the large classes she would place each one. I soon worked it out that if I kept Bliss standing perfectly while she continued judging the rest of the class I might stay at the top of the line up. We did not relax for one minute and in its turn every Beagle bitch was compared with Bliss who remained first and the other bitches were placed behind her.

She also won in her second class and I could not have been more delighted and proud. A single first win at Crufts was a marvellous achievement, and we had won two firsts. Later during the day a Swedish Specialist breeder offered me 150 Guineas for Bliss, of course I did not accept.

Eventually the business my husband managed was moved to Leys Avenue, Letchworth, and the owner purchased a house for us, the house we moved into had a large garden ample space for the dogs.

Both Carol and Jean had passed their exams to go to Letchworth school, so they did not have far to walk. They had made so many friends and had a lot of interests so my dog activities did not interfere with their education and pleasure.

Jean received an excellent report from the school, both my husband and I wanted her to stay at school and take more exams, and then perhaps go on even further with her education, but as it was Jean and her boyfriend Roger had plans of their own they were married at St. Gabriel Church in Letchworth on 8th September 1965, and setup their home in Stotfold. A few years later their children Emma and Matthew were born.

Carol eventually left Letchworth Grammar school and

Blithesome 6 weeks old

First Beagle litter from Cornevon Blithesome

Joyce, Teddy & Sally, Golden Retrievers

Lady Sally of Theydon

Carol and Neils wedding

Jean and Rogers wedding

Carol at College

Jean on holiday

took further education at St. Gabriel College when she left she met Neil and they were married 28th July 1965, she was also a daughter to be proud of. She also had two children, Sacha and Leon. Today she is a teacher who has written three books on Dislectic children and adults, she also gives lectures on that subject.

A friend contacted me to say that he had a litter of very nice Golden Retrievers and I purchased a bitch named Lady Sally of Theydon, when she was two years old I decided to have a litter from her and as it was my first Golden Retriever litter I kept a handsome male dog and called him Adam.

Unfortunately at six months I saw he was not entire. I could not show Adam, nor breed from him, so I contacted Mr. Brown, a farmer friend who had Adam's litter brother. He agreed to exchange dogs and said that I could pick him up on Saturday. On Friday he called me to say that his dog got out and got hit by a car and both his legs were broken so he had to keep him to give him the care he needed.

It seemed as if bad luck was following me as Sally was chasing a hare on a freshly ploughed field and broke both front legs. She was retired and eventually died of old age.

I bought a Golden Retriever puppy sired by one of the top winning dogs of the time Ch. Simon of Westley. Her pet name was Teddy. She was gorgeous, everything I would want in a litter from her later. I showed her several times and won firsts, then to top that we won Best of Breed and a Trophy. I thought my bad luck was changing, then it happened. I took Teddy to a local field to exercise regularly as she loved the freedom and looked forward to her walk, one day I noticed that she looked dazed then she dropped to the ground and rolled down the hill. I rushed after her, picked her up and carried her to the car. I immediately took her to the Vet who checked her and told me she had Meningitis and would continue like that for a while. He gave me medicine for her and I took her home. Her condition lasted over two weeks and she was getting no better. It broke my heart to see lovely Teddy unable to stand, and she could only take food from my hand eventually I gave in and had her put to sleep to avoid further suffering.

I was now spending more time showing Beagles and Golden Retrievers at Championship shows, so I decided to register an Affix with the Kennel Club. The combination of Beagles and Golden Retrievers gave me the idea of choosing BEAGOLD as my Affix.

Time passed by and I had entered both the Beagle and the Golden Retriever at Richmond Championship show. The Beagles were on the ground floor and the Goldens were on the second floor. I somehow got lost, and ended up near the Bearded Collie ring. I did not know the name of the breed but was fascinated by their behaviour. Not one of them looked like a well groomed show dog, except one that was in the Open class, I later found out that he was owned by Miss Lynne Evans, Heathermead Handsome. Sally was never mated again, and I did not take her to shows very often. When she was 12 years old she just went to sleep peacefully on her bed and did not wake up. The Beagles other than Bliss could not settle at our home in the centre of town so I decided to give them to Mrs Gibson who lived out in the country. I continued to show Bliss, and in the Beagle classes at Windsor that I was in the line up with Mrs. Catherine Sutton later to become famous for the Rossut Beagles, and world renowned as a famous International judge of all breeds. Sadly now many of the old Beagle famous faces have gone from the show ring, many have died and others have retired.

Acquiline Golden Teddy

Lady Sally of Theydon and first litter

TERRIERS AND GUNDOGS

I had always been friendly with the RSPCA Inspector who lived in the next town, one day he phoned to say he was collecting a four month old Kerry Blue Terrier that was not wanted by the owners. He agreed that the dog was boisterous and did not look much as it had never been groomed. I decided then and there that I would try to give the dog a home to save it from being put down. My friend was right it was boisterous, and it stank like a goat, which is why the ideal name that I chose for him was McGinty. I bathed and combed him, this must have been the first time he had been clean and the shock kept him quiet while I worked. I had no experience of stripping Terriers so phoned a friend who had West Highland Whites, Dorothy Farnham was an expert at grooming all breeds of Terriers, but I think she found McGinty a real challenge. I held him while she stripped his coat down and before long we both could recognize that he was a good looking dog, with his coat styled he definitely showed potential, in fact I though he would be good enough to be trained for the show ring.

This seemed an impossible task, when I first had him he had never been on a lead and did not cooperate at all with any restriction on his movement. His pedigree was excellent with several well known Champions as his sire and grandsires. When he was just over six months I entered him for an Open show, he did not disgrace me or his ancestors, he behaved perfectly and won his class. We progressed to Championship shows and then to Crufts. McGinty won a third at Crufts, which is a prize to be treasured at such a prestigious show, I was very proud of him. I enjoyed groom-

McGinty, Kerry Blue Terrier

ing him and he seemed to enjoy the attention. We went to several shows and he won well, I could only foresee a bright future for McGinty. He was kennelled on his own as I was never quite sure he would not be aggressive towards another dog. Some Terriers can be aggressive.

Then tragedy struck again at the Beagold kennels. McGinty was 3 years old and with very few Kerry bitches in the area I was delighted to have a stud request from another well known breeder who lived in Norfolk. It never came to pass. McGinty had a large window in his sleeping quarters and he saw a dog pass by his window, very excited he jumped at the window, which shattered, cutting himself very badly by the time we had got him to the Vet he lost so much blood and died. I was broken hearted, I loved all my dogs, but having to spend so much time with the Scissors and grooming McGinty to prepare him for the shows I had grown to admire his super character and loving ways, his temperament with me was exemplary, even if he did have a go at other dogs. I shall always remember him with affection.

A friend living near by had bred a litter of Sussex Spaniels she had told me that the breed was nearly extinct as there had been so few Sussex bred successfully for many years. To help reestablish the breed she had mated brother to sister. She said she would be grateful if I agreed to take a puppy dog from the litter. While he was young there was no problem at all. He was a very handsome young dog, but as he grew older I noticed that he had a temperament problem. I named him Richard he was fine with me but would rush out and frighten friends who came to visit. He never bit anyone at that time, I made sure of that but his aggressive attitude was frightening. I took him to a show and the judge bent over to go over his body but I was worried the judge's face was very near to Richard's mouth, and if he wanted to he could have snapped. Mr. Douglas Appleton had a beard and Richard had never seen anyone so close with a beard and he was fascinated. He was placed second in the class but my nerves could not stand the tension again.

So I left him out of the show ring. His temperament got worst and his breeders decided that it would be wisest to have him put down, they were not happy about losing their good name. The Sussex Spaniel breeders all decided to bring in the Clumber Spaniel bloodline to help the breed increase in numbers and improve in temperament. A very sensible plan proved by the quality and temperament in the breed which has improved immensely in later years.

I was so upset to loose Richard, I vowed not to take

McGinty just groomed

Sussex Spaniel Richard

sympathy on any more different breeds.

As I had spent many years showing my Beagles, Golden Retrievers and Kerry Blues etc. I decided to register a prefix with the kennel Club. The combination of both Beagles and Golden Retrievers would be shortened to BEAGOLD. That meant that for every dog I bred or owned would carry the prefix of BEAGOLD. My main ambition from my early days was to start a judging career. I was starting at the very bottom to learn. I had a very large library of good dog books, and for many years I had spent most of my free time reading about the various Kennel Club Standards of all breeds. Whenever I had the chance I would discuss with fellow exhibitors the finer points of their dogs and having a retentive memory it would stand me in good stead in the future.

I use to travel by coach to the long distance shows and especially when we travelled to Scotland I was able to see Champions and BOB winners with their owners on the coach. The expense of going was all taken into my plan for a judging career. Such a long distance would usually only attract those people who owned top quality show dogs, knowing that they had more of a chance to win.

Before long I was asked to organize Exemption shows myself so many amusing instances come to mind. A very good friend of mine agreed to judge, although she was a qualified Championship judge, she agreed that it was a good caused, so she would be willing to help raise money. She agreed to judge the Pedigree and Novelty classes. I received a telephone call the evening before the show from a lady who wanted to know had I got an experienced judge for the show. I explained that she was very experience of all breeds, and judged regularly at Open and Championship Shows. She then asked who was the Novelty judge. I told her it was to be the same judge. I then asked her what breed of dog was she bringing. To my amazement she said proudly “he is a Mongrel, and I hope your judge is familiar with Mongrels."

At the same show I had some very experienced people who organized the Obedience side of the show. A lady phoned to ask what classes the Obedience organizers were classifying. I explained that the new KC rules were that they must not call the classes the same as those at an Open show. So the classes that would be at the Exemption show would be called Class 1. Triers, Class 2. Knocking Knees, Class 3. Hopefuls, Class 4. Show Offs. The lady said, " Oh dear my dog will not work in those different named classes, he is use to working with Open show correctly named classes." I suggested that she did not let the dog 'read scheduled program'!!, but tell him that it was Pre-beginners, Novice, Beginners and Open classes that he was entered in and perhaps he would agree to work.

I had a most enjoyable ten years as Secretary of Hitchin Dist. C.S. So many happy days and most unusual experiences. The work of Secretary is very demanding and I had to resign from being Secretary of the dog obedience club, although I continued to train my own dogs whenever possible. We held our shows at the Hitchin Town Hall, which was situated in the centre of Hitchin, this always gave us parking problems also there were no special exercise areas for the dogs. We did set aside a small area for the dogs to relieve themselves, but thoughtless exhibitors took their dogs along the back roads, and it was not long before we had many complaints that dog show exhibitors were allowing their dogs to mess along the grammar school walk. The head mistress complained and we had to move. I found a hall further out of town that needed a regular income, so they made us welcome.

One episode that I find hard to forget is that I received a telephone call from the Secretary of the Kennel Club. It was a few days after Crufts, and the German Television people had come to televise Crufts, and they also wanted to include a smaller dog show in their program, we happened to be the only society that had booked a show that same week. The film was going to be called, “The biggest dog show and the smallest dog show”. The Kennel Club asked me to put on a special show for the visitors, I had three days to organize it. On Monday I booked the judge, I was very pleased to get her as she spoke German which would be a great help when it came to entertaining the TV crew. I phoned around telling members that their presence would definitely be needed and they all responded well. Tuesday morning I heard the fire engines go past our home and I casually looked out to see where they were going, I could not believe my eyes, the hall was on fire. Smoke and flames bellowed out of the doors and windows, even with the immediate attention of the fire brigade it would be impossible to hold a show at the venue the next day.

As luck would have it I was able to book a converted barn in Ashwell. Then I had to inform all the exhibitors and the judge of the new venue. The German TV crew were delighted with the barn, and did not want any thing altered, in fact they brought in bales of straw for us to sit on, the modern chairs that we had begged for were taken away. The bar was hidden from view with more bales of straw. They put up old farm implements around the walls and brought in beer barrels from the local public house, obviously to make it look like we were beer drinkers. They took down all the modern pictures then set up their cameras. When the exhibitors started arriving they asked them to park their cars in another car park, and they photographed all the exhibitors walking across the fields with their dogs. They had a huge sign printed “DOG SHOW” no doubt the commentator would say to his German audience “The English dog owners walk miles on foot to their dog shows in the country”.

With the TV film as evidence, I am sure the Germans would believe what they were shown. It was a super show and everyone joined in the charade, if there was more than the usual fun and laughter during the show of the funny antics of the TV crew who did their best to show the German viewers a typical efficiently organized dog show, if there was anything they did not understand they would put it down to the unusual British humour.

While I was Secretary I sent dates of the next shows to the local newspaper reporters, I had to setup situations of unusual happenings and arrange photographs that would be used for the front page giving me a free advertisement for each of our shows. The dog exhibitors are an eccentric group of people and the papers would have had a field day if they decided to come regularly to every show. One exhibitor who came regularly to our show was a professional breeder and handler of Bulldogs, and it was not surprising that the photographers soon saw the resemblance of owner and dog. George Wakefield, sadly no longer with us had a round chubby face, lined with laughter lines, and smoked a cigar like Winston Churchill, wore a Deerstalker hat which gave the impression that he had ears like his dog. His Bulldog had the same expression, and George happily let them photograph him in so many different poses with his dog.

Whenever we had a Wolfhound or Bloodhound come to the show it was a foregone conclusion that it would be photographed with a tiny Chihuahua, and the caption would read "Big brother is watching you".

My rescued Kerry Blue, McGinty, took the head lines for several editions, and his photograph appeared with the caption "Doomed dog wins two more trophies" and "McGinty on his way to Crufts".

As Secretary it usually fell to my lot to organize exemption shows for charity. The exhibitors would always rally around and support the shows. It was difficult to find a venue, as no one could rely on good weather in a typical British summer. I wanted all the proceeds to go to the chosen charity so I did not want to pay rent for a hall. I persuaded the Harkness Rose Garden owners in Letchworth to allow us to have a show in their expensive grounds. The Harkness brothers were most helpful and the show started with a huge entry where the exhibitors took advantage to see the magnificent display of roses and plants after they had completed their classes.

Unfortunately before the show was half way through huge black clouds gathered and the rain poured down, the only shelter was the nearby empty green houses. Fortunately it was early summer and they were not being used. Although it was raining the heat in the green houses was intense, but the marvellous dog show exhibitors took the unusual venue all in their stride, and I received not one complaint even though they were continually wiping the sweat from their brows. The reporters had a field day with the situation and the headlines read “the first time a dog show was held in a green house”. Not everyone was pleased with the arrangement of a dog show in the Harkness green houses, even though they were empty of all flowers.

The head gardener saw all the dogs and owners arrive so he came to look for me and in a very crossed voice he said, “if any of your people slash my water pipes with their knives I will report you to the police” if I was not so surprised at his remarks I would have laughed at him, but I explained quietly, “I don’t think that dog exhibitors carry knives for any reason, but I will certainly inform them of your concern”. I thought it advisable not to mention the head gardener’s problems concerning his water pipes to the Harkness brothers.

Because I made it my policy to feed information to the newspaper reporters, knowing that it would give me free advertisement for future shows, when I attended Crufts this was a news worthy subject that could not be missed, in fact they even sent a reporter to travel with me on the coach. This was a very good idea when I thought I would be placed in the classes with my dogs.

But this year it was not a very good idea as my dogs won nothing. Not to be out done with their reports they put a photograph of me with my two dogs, sitting on the bench at Crufts, and the caption read "priceless but cheerful" I have suffered for years when friends saw that spelling error.

Garfield Moonlight my first Beardie and Ch Beagold Ella at Crufts 1965.
"Priceless but cheerful"

INTRODUCTION TO THE BEARDED COLLIE

I was at Richmond Championship Show and it was the year that they had Golden Retrievers on the ground floor and the Beagles upstairs. I had taken both breeds not knowing that they were on different floor levels. I spent the whole day running up the stairs to show the Beagles, then dashing downstairs to get my Golden Retriever into her class. I got lost on one journey and found my attention drawn to a breed that was being shown, that I had never seen before.

I was very interested to watch, with no stretch of the imagination could it be classified as a trained show dog type. It was of medium size, very shaggy, with different shades of grey, black and brown in their makeup. It looked a fun dog, its character was evident, as it first stood for inspection then like a spring it charged across the ring, pleased to be moving. I was fascinated to watch and to learn what breed it was. This was my first sight of the Bearded Collie, and I realized with that wonderful character and friendly lively outlook on life it would make a wonderful companion there was one dog in the Open Dog class that drew my attention. He was a handsome fellow, and so well behaved, and of course he won the class and BOB. His owner was a young girl, who obviously loved her dog, the rapport between them showed as the dog watched her every move with adoring and attentive expression.

From that time onwards I gathered all the information I could about the Bearded Collie. It was 1963 and only a

Beagold Black Camaro

few Bearded Collies were being shown. I learnt that Mrs. Willison was the owner of the Bothkennar Beardies, and sometimes had puppies for sale. I phoned her and she told me that she did have a litter, I must send her a deposit and she would save a puppy for me as they were six weeks old. I asked if I could come to see the litter and I would give her a deposit while I was there. She refused, saying that she had many calls about her puppies and if I was not willing to let her pick one for me I could not have one. With that autocratic remark I decided to search elsewhere. I had always been satisfied when I picked my own puppy from a litter, I was willing to learn but there was a nicer way of speaking to a person that was willing to spend money.

Later I heard of a litter for sale by Miss Morris, the stud dog was Ch. Bosky Glen Of Bothkennar (litter brother to Ch. Bravo Of Bothkennar) out of her Swalehall Martha Scrope. Miss Morris was a charming lady and invited a friend and me down to see the puppies, and to stay for lunch. I picked a very attractive black/white bitch puppy called Ailsa, the litter had not been registered with the Kennel Club so later I changed her name to Beagold Ella. We had lunch and I carried my precious burden home. My Goldens had all passed away and I only had one old Beagle left so I had space for another breed.

I was captivated with the Bearded Collie and the next person I contacted for a puppy was Mrs. Banks, owner of the Gayfield Kennels. She had a fawn bitch for sale called Gayfield Moonlight. I should have been wary of buying a Beardie from those kennels but I was so keen to get Ella a companion that I overlooked the well known wildness of her dogs and bitches. While I was there they snapped and snarled at the wire fence between their runs, but I was assured that it was playful behaviour. Moonlight was quiet on the journey home and seemed to settle in quite nicely, she did not take to Ella, but I thought they would get used to each other and be friends. That was my mistake. They were exercising in the field and for no reason at all Moonlight jumped on Ella and I had to part them before they drew blood. I had warned Mrs Banks that if she did not settle I would bring her back, Mrs. Banks agreed.

She had quite a few Beardies of different ages running about so I imaged that others had been returned owing to aggressive behaviour.

My next choice was a super tempered dog called Jayemji Derhue bred by Mrs. Foster. His pet name was Derry, he settled in very well. I could not wait to take him to shows as he developed into a really handsome dog. Ella also had good show potential so I spent time show training them both.

With their long coat I was very busy continually grooming them. Both had excellent temperament so life looked very rosy for my introduction into the Bearded Collie world.

When going to a show you leave the house with two perfectly groomed Bearded Collies. Time and time again I had to carry each dog from the car to the benches in the tents as the rains created muddy ground at the venues. I was very pleased to learn about the Vetzyme grooming company, which was originally owned by Mrs. Willison, their first product had a logo which included 'Jeannie Of Bothkennar' advertising their goods. They brought out a new product around 1968, which was Vetzyme Foam Shampoo. This was the early foam product that sprayed onto the white parts of the Beardie coats, rubbed in then towelled dry, this left the white parts white and sparkling. I found it very useful and always took a can of the foam with me to shows. At one show I carried my Beardie while I jumped from tussock to tussock trying to stay out of the sodden ground. Then I arrived on a small island and found the only way to keep my feet dry was to retreat with my burden, who was getting quite restive and wanted to get down, then along came another exhibitor who saw my plight and took the Beardie from my arms and carried him through the mud and water to higher ground. The very kind 'Sir Walter Raleigh' had on Wellington boots, I thanked him profusely as he did not need to help me. Then I set to work with my Vetzyme Foam Shampoo and my Beardie did not look quite so bad as some of the others. My prefix BEAGOLD worked well as I went into Bearded Collies, the first three letters were the same as Beagles.

The following year at Crufts the Vetzyme people had a very flattering photo of me advertising their Vetzyme Foam Shampoo large enough to attract much attention again. I had been asked to wear white so I chose a white jumper, a brown and black striped shirt and I knelt down with my two Beardies. I had Jayemji Derrhie and his son from Beagold

Jayemji Derhue on the advert for Players Gold Leaf Cigarettes

Ella, both dogs had snow white paws and shirt front, both dogs had very black body coats, and in the back ground was the white marquee to emphasise that anyone using the shampoo would look like us.

A month or two later I was contacted by the Tony Stone studios in London, asking me if I would bring one of my Beardies along to be photographed with over a hundred other dogs as they wanted to find a suitable dog to advertise Gold Leaf Cigarettes. It was fun and both Derry and I enjoyed these photograph sessions where we joined in a completely different world from our quiet country life. We arrived at the studio where there were several other dogs of different breeds, they were obviously going to have photographic sessions over several days. Our turn came and we were invited into the studio proper. There was a very handsome young man sitting on a stool, dressed in black. I had to encourage Derry to go to the young man and be friendly, Derry loved everyone so that was not a hard task, then he was encouraged to half sit on the young man's lap and look into his face. This again proved something that Derry was quite happy to do. The only thing was the young man did not like Derry's hair dropping onto his black outfit. It made me wonder why he had taken on the job, even the best kept dogs shed a few hairs when under hot arc lights. I had been told if they were interested we would be contacted.

Three weeks went by then I received a phone call Derry had been chosen from over a hundred dogs to advertise the Gold Leaf Cigarettes, a car would be sent to pick us up to go to the studio in London.

Of course I agreed, and when we arrived we were treated like royalty slightly different from the previous visit. I was shown the rough proofs of Derry with the young man and they looked superb.

This time the photos would be taken by the top American photographer, Mr. Richard Avadon.

We sat down to wait. The door opened and in came Richard Avadon with his entourage he swept in and smiled at us, I could not believe my eyes he was dressed in Mauve velvet, with a mauve sombrero type hat. Derry was already groomed so we went into the main studio where Derry greeted everyone and especially the male model who seemed to be a dog lover. The clothes he wore were checked against Derry's coat for colour, from a huge rail several jumpers and suits were put against Derry's coat.

Finally they were satisfied his outfit matched the colour of Derry's coat. The model sat on the floor and I was told to put Derry between his legs that were stretched out in front of him. He quite happily sat between the model's legs, put one of his paws on his knee and gazed up into his face with a most beautiful expression. They took a shot and then so many others as the model was supposed to hold the cigarette smoking in his hand as well as the packet. This went on for hours, and each time the cigarette burned more than a quarter of an inch before it was taken away and another placed in his hand. It was hot and tiring work but the only one not affected by the delays and the heat was Derry. At last Richard Avadon called a halt when he said that he had enough photos to choose some good ones from.

I got very involved with the Bearded Collie breed and was very pleased when invited to go onto the Bearded Collie Club committee, who held their meetings at the Paddington West Hall Hotel in London. Several of the members were keen to persuade Mrs. Willison, the President, to write her Bothkennar story as she had been talking about retiring completely and we were all very sad that her story would be lost forever. The history of the Bearded Collie had been restored by Mrs. Willison. Betty Foster, the breeder of my Jayemji Derhues suggested to the committee that I contact Mrs. Willison and ask if I could help her write the book on the Bearded Collie. I had writing experience by providing articles for the dog magazines and I had also written a chapter on Bearded Collies for Mr. and Mrs. Cartledge's book on Collies.

I wrote to Mrs. Willison, and after one or two exchanges of letters she agreed to accept my help. I was to send her questions etc., about the Beardie and she would fill in the answers. From very interesting pages of answers I was able to compile a manuscript to be sent to a publisher of her choice.

I suggested that the book should be headed the 'Bothkennar Story', which it really was as she was the person who restored interest in the breed and the content in this book would be treasured by future generations of Bearded Collie owners. It was a difficult undertaking for me to work with Mrs. Willison, and I was never told why the title was changed to 'Bearded Collie'. It may have been suggested by the publishers Foyles who were producing a series of different books with the names of the breeds used as the titles rather than the names of writers.

I still have the original papers with my typing questions and Mrs. Willison's answers and additions. When I asked her why she had not written the book herself her answer was, "I was too busy with the breeding programme and since my nervous breakdown in 1963 I have been unable to concentrate sufficiently to write a book".

I was disappointed to learn that the publisher was Foyles. I had hoped that she would let me recommend my publisher Pelham books. We would have been able to fill the whole book with her story instead of the rest of the book being taken up with standard information as in all other breeds concerning health, feeding, illness and training, all good information in its own right, but not the full story and information that Mrs. Willison wanted to pass on and is still saught after today. Several years later Foyles book publishers had contacted me to revise the Bearded Collie book but I had to refuse because I was in the process of writing a Bearded Collie book for Pelham books.

The complete running of the Kennels was my responsibility. George would feed the dogs when I was away judging. So I had to keep a limited number of dogs. I was judging in Finland and noticed a beautiful tri coloured dog, I enquired the name of the breed and was told they were Bernese Mountain dogs and as they moved around the ring in unison it made a handsome sight, I had never seen the breed in the show ring in England so was very interested to make enquiries about them.

I heard that a breeder of Mastiffs also had imported Bernese Mt. Dogs. She had a litter at the present time, all the puppies had been booked with only one dog left which she intended to keep. But because of circumstances at the time, and there was a telephone strike, she had to change her mind and the puppy dog was for sale. I went to view him, he was the most super pup, with an outstanding temperament.

As a puppy I took him to several shows and each time he won, I entered him at Richmond Championship Show, little did I know that he would cause such great interest. His excellent unusual markings, his size and temperament also caused an interest to the Reporters around the ring, which upset the judge. Although he must have been pleased with the dog as he awarded him a qualifying prize for Crufts 1971.

The trouble continued as the Reporters also arrived at Crufts which made the judge Mr. Warner Hill, one of the most influential judges very annoyed with all the fuss that was made by the Reporters coming into the ring. Mr. Warner Hill came over to me and said, “You have to get out of my ring as you are making my ring into a Circus”. I left with Bernie so he was not judged at all.

Bernie always caused a great interest at all the shows we went to. I was sitting on the bench beside him at a show in Wales. Several people came to see him as he was the only one of his breed there. One particular man stood in front of us admiring him. He said, “He is a handsome huge dog, he must cost you a lot to feed him.” I agreed with him and replied, “Yes he eats a lot, I am always making love to my butcher”. I suddenly realized what a silly remark I had made. He laughed and said, “I am a butcher, I have a steak here in my pocket for my dinner tonight but you can have it”. I was so embarrassed but we enjoyed the joke as did all the people standing around who heard the conversation.

As Bernie was winning at the shows so much I realized that the owners of his relations were getting jealous. A friend who was benched next to us warned me never to leave my dog on his own, as someone might do him harm.

Because of all the jealousy I let Bearnie go to America to

a friend, Mr Dick Schneider who promised to come to England to collect him. Bernie was also HD clear and because of this I had received a letter from breeders in Switzerland asking me to let him come to their country as he would be a great asset to them as a stud dog.

Dick Schneider arrived in England with a huge crate to pick him up. When they arrived at Kennedy Airport, he fed and gave him water, then went into the airport to sign and collect the papers, when he returned to Bernie the cage door was open and there was no sign of the dog. Dick phoned me and said that a baggage attendant had opened the door to pet the dog and Bernie ran away, he was going to sue the airport for the loss of the dog. I was broken hearted. Nine months later Dick found Bernie at a disused Car Lot near the Airport.

Bernie was not in a good state. Bernie was nursed back to health and was able to attend a few shows, sadly the following year in the very hot summer Bernie died. I let him go to America, I thought he would be safe there, but I was wrong.

Back in 1968 as Secretary of the Hitchin and Dist. CS. I received a phone call from an American serving here with the US military asking for directions to the venue of the coming show. Over the years we kept in touch and in 1976, the American Felix Cosme, who had retired from the US military wrote to say he was coming to live in England eventually, and hoped to be involved in the dog world in England. He was a Professional GSD handler in New York, he also showed his own German Shepherd. While still in the military he had attended a course on military Patrol Dog and drug detection, mainly with German Shepherds. He wanted to be introduced to the German Shepherd exhibitors in the UK.

Another milestone in my life with the Beardies was when I was invited to America in 1975 to meet Mr. Bill Stifle, the American kennel Club representative who was there to see if the Beardie should be recognized for inclusion onto the American Register. The show was at Mt. Kisco, NY. Where I also judged the breed. They had arranged for a Scottish Piper to play Amazing Grace to lead me onto the showground. There was a complete mixture of types as the Americans had imported Beardies from so many different kennels in the UK, and at that time we had also a variety of types here but we had a larger gene pool. The Americans were exhibiting a variety of the imported dogs and bitches, even a completely white Bearded Collie imported from Scotland, who later became a champion. The breed had been accepted on the American register before they had compiled a standard, so the owners of the white Beardie were not happy when the colour, all white was not accepted.

My husband had decided to purchase a much larger property and intended to increase his activities to wholesale and retail business while running his own shop. So we moved into another large building in Letchworth. Both daughters were doing very well at grammar school and involved with their many friends.

The numbers of Bearded Collies was increasing in numbers everywhere. I was honoured to be invited to judge the first Open show of the National Working Breeds inaugural show that classified the Bearded Collie. Then I was invited to judge the breed at Crufts in 1980.

After judging Bearded Collies at Crufts 1980, I received so many judging appointments abroad. I was so pleased when the invitation included several other breeds that I was qualified to judge.

One particular country that I was very delighted to visit to judge was Switzerland. I had been in contact with Jeanne Trevisanne who lived in Staffa near Zurich. She had bought a Bearded Collie puppy from me, I said I would bring the puppy with me on the journey and stay with her for a weeks holiday. She said she would introduce me to

Left: Bill Stifel, Secretary of the American Kennel Club

Below left: Her Honor

Below right: Frae Bonnie Scotland playing 'Amazing Grace'

the committee of the Zurich Kennel Club.

I arrived at Zurich airport at 2pm, and had to wait for my case and the puppy in a crate to arrive. My case came up through the floor then banged heavily onto the conveyor belt. I had horrible vision of the poor puppy in her travelling box popping up through the floor. Thank goodness the two porters came directly from the plane wheeling the puppy in her crate on a trolley. She was sleepy from the journey, but immediately she saw me she wagged her tail and started barking.

Jeanne and her husband Umberto were delighted with the pup and took us to the car. We travelled sixteen miles from Zurich to their home in Staffa. It was dark and I could not see the scenery, but the fresh air sweet and clean told me we were in Switzerland. Next morning Jeanne's pretty little curly brown haired two year old came with us on a walk. The magnificent scenery was just like you would see in the picture books. No fences, hedges or gates separated us from the gardens or orchards, we could have picked the delicious red apples from the bright green trees, every house on our journey up the hills from Staffa had window boxes ablaze with brightly coloured flowers.

The next day Jeanne and I took Haggis her dog up into the hills to her dog training school. A huge lake could be seen in the distance surrounded by mountains. On another hill I could see a small aeroplane flying club. The small planes looked like toys in the bright blue sky up above. The Swiss have made good use of their beautiful hills, quite often pupils from the local riding school waved to us as they rode by. On the way home a herd of cows crossed our path, free to graze anywhere they chose to go. The huge bells that hung from their neck warned us of their approach.

We were due to take Haggis to Austria the next day. Unfortunately a Fox had been killed the previous week and the Vet warned everyone that it had died of Rabies.

Enjoying my first meal in Switzerland

Dog Training School in Switzerland

It was a great disappointment because we could not take Haggis with us to the show.

It was a magnificent journey to Austria to the show one that I will never forget. One the way Umberto picked up Anne Kurzvain one of the top Bearded Collie breeders in Switzerland. When we arrived at the show I was surprised to see it was mainly setup in several different streets a roped off area, with a large umbrella shading the Secretary from the sun. I could not follow the setup as it was so completely different to the other shows I had been to. Terriers, Non-Sporting and Toys were all being judged in the same ring most of the men were dressed in a sort of uniform a bright green jacket with bright red lining and embroidered trousers many had typical Austrian hats.

The next day Umberto said he would take me to a different kennels and on the way we would pickup Anne Kuzbein again as she was due to go to a kennel club committee meeting in Berne. I was very interested in the Siberian Husky kennels where huge exercise areas had been allocated to twenty dogs I noticed that the dogs were recycling their manure. The kennel manager explained to me that the Siberian Huskies were reverting to their wild instinct. We also went to a Rough Collie kennel the dogs were all for show I was told but I considered that they were a very mixed variety of quality dogs so I was not too impressed.

We arrived at Berne and drew up outside a huge impressive high quality class hotel. I followed them in to a beautiful decorated dining room. As we walked into the room everyone stood up and started clapping, I was led to the top table and all the officials greeted me, they all were beautifully dressed, and as I shook hands with them I could see that they all had on Zurich committee badges. The empty seat beside one gentleman had a tray on the table with a cup and saucer, tea pot, and sugar basin. I had a horrible feeling that it was my place, and I was certainly not suitably dressed to be a guest of honour. I was introduced as a judge from the English Kennel Club, before I could correct the speaker he went on talking in a language which I did not understand.

After a few minutes there was clapping again and I was beckoned to stand up and talk. I said a few words in English to Umberto, knowing if I had made a faux pas he would have corrected it. More clapping then I was pointed to my tray of tea. Never before or since have I been watched so closely pouring out a cup of tea by so many.

WE MOVE TO LEYS AVENUE

NO sooner had we moved into the building in Leys Avenue, with the shop downstairs, and a large two story flat above, with 4 bedrooms. My mother in-law was invited by my husband to come and stay with us. I imagined it would be for a week or two, but the weeks, months and even a year went by. The only good thing for me was I had more freedom to attend more dog shows. I worked in the shop daily, and when floral orders came in some times I had to make wreaths and wedding bouquets late into the night. My daughters had many friends, and other interests and were both busy at school. Husband, wife and both daughters were very happy to go there separate ways throughout the year.

At one time I was on thirteen dog show committees, and enjoying every one of them. I was judging several breeds, Groups and Best in show. I was delighted to be invited to judge at the Championship shows by the breeds I was qualified to do so.

As I mentioned before, my first overseas judging appointment was at Mt. Kisko, New York where I judged the Bearded Collie championship show in 1975.

From then on judging appointments abroad came my way often, the longest distance I had to travel was to New Zealand and then onto Australia. At most shows abroad I was asked to give lectures as the audience enjoyed listening about our dogs in England, and the question time went on far into the night. When judging in Australia all day then enjoying the barbecue, then giving a lecture, I certainly earned my keep especially when there was another breed at another show to judge the next day.

We thought we had settled but only a few years went by before we were moving again.

My husband was working from early morning to late at night, and his health was suffering, his doctor advised him to retire. So he purchased a de licensed Public House with plenty of ground in the country. I hoped he would take notice of the doctor's advice. He was a workaholic and always had been. It was a lovely country home and I was very pleased that George took up gardening, I was so relieved that at last he was taking notice of the warning words that he must rest more.

I was so pleased to receive a letter from Felix Cosme again, I had met him at the show in 1968 when he was stationed in England at the RAF base at High Wycombe. He had now retired from the US Navy and was returning to England, and hoped to renew our friendship. I was pleased to offer him a partnership in the Beagold Kennels, which he accepted. His German Shepherd had died of old age and he was free to handle and show my dogs. I told him that other dog owners would be keen to use his expertise in handling.

Felix lived with us, and not only did he help me with the kennels, he helped my husband and provided male companionship for him, especially when he was feeling ill.

It was a great upset for us all when we had to call the ambulance urgently as George was having a heart attack. He was rushed into hospital over Christmas and when he came home he was warned, that he would be called to undergo a heart operation at Harefield heart hospital in London as soon as a bed became available.

My husband George was not a person to accept sympathy or help, and certainly it was never in his mind to take life easy. He would come into the house in the evening and collapse in his arm chair exhausted. I know I would be wasting my time if I suggested that the next day he would be sensible and stay in the house for a rest. His doctor would not believe that he spent the whole day everyday in his garden digging, planting, and attempting all sorts of heavy work.

Felix my Manager and Beagold Porter Harvey (Photo: North Herts Gazette)

After a strong storm we lost some tiles from the roof. I immediately telephoned a workman to come to repair the damage. He agreed but said he was very busy but would come in two days time.

I arrived home from a shopping expedition and tried to find George in the house. Knowing he was not well it was always a great worry when he went missing. Then I went outside and saw Felix at the bottom of the ladder, and George on the roof mending the tiles. Felix said he felt bad that George would not let him go up the ladder as George said he was to heavy and he must stay at the bottom of the ladder to hold it safe. George would not admit that he suffered pain for several days later after climbing on the roof.

Life seemed to settled down for a while as George was taking life easier. I was very amused when nearly every day George would mark the articles on politics in the Times newspaper. Felix was not a reader at all, as he said to a lady in Norway when she asked him had he read the book on the History of Norway, and he answered, "If its not about dogs, I am sorry but I am sure I have not read it", but George continued with marking the paper for his homework.

A few months went by as I was having a committee meeting in the dinning room, George was in the lounge watching television. Suddenly we were all shocked to hear a loud cry of pain from him. We all rushed to see what had happened to find he was having another heart attack. Felix immediately called for the ambulance. When they arrived and examined George, they said I must pack a case for him to be taken to hospital. As usual George complained that the pain he was having in his chest was only indigestion, and we were fussing him as usual and he did not want to go to hospital. The ambulance men ignored his plea and took him to hospital. He had several attacks while there, and several days later he passed away.

After fifty years of being married to George I had to somehow get used to not helping him run various Green Grocery Shops that he managed, and at times being on my own taking care of the shops while he drove to the different farms and various markets. Over the years it seemed he had a low regard for resting, as he worked all hours of the day and sometimes at night. Sadly his down fall, health wise was his ability to succeed so well in the wholesale business, he was in great demand by those who owned the shops, always enabling him to have a managerial position until he had saved enough money to purchase his own Green Grocery shop, but instead of taking things easier as an owner, he worked even harder until ill health caught up with him. Because of this I immersed myself with the various doggy and judging activities while allowing Felix the running of the kennels on his own.

By this time I was a dedicated Bearded Collie exhibitor, I enjoyed grooming them and they enjoyed being groomed. When I had my first litter from Ella by my dog Derry I was fascinated with the odd one out, a very pretty well marked blue and white which I planned to sell, but it turned out to be a beautiful show dog with blue coat, blue pigment and dove grey blue eye colour which at the time was not a well known colour. A few years later Mrs. Jenny Osborne campaigned Ch. Bonnie Blue Braid who at that time was the top dog winning most of the CC's on offer, a dog of Blue colouring.

The standard for the Bearded Collie has always held a fascination for me, ever since I helped Mrs. Willison write her book for Foyles. She was adamant when it came to the four colours of the breed. I have always agreed with her remarks, "Bearded Collies are born with only four recognized colours, black, brown, blue, and fawn," she suggested when writing a critique after judging, it is wise to mention the correct variety of colours in a grey dog as born black. To distinguish it from the born blue, as the born blue should have dove grey blue eyes as called for in the standard.

A most amusing but important occurrence made me remember very well those colours when I was showing my Beardie at a Championship show at Richmond many years ago. The judge, no longer with us was trying to show that he was familiar with the breed he was judging, and the steward was trying to help him write his critique. He had judged most of his classes and put B (for colours) in each class. His steward asked me to help check which dogs he had placed whether they were black, brown or blue.

Most judges do remark on the colour of the coat when describing the Beardie in their critique as the standard dictates the proper colour, but now newcomers to the breed have brought in the colour SLATE. Another modern change in the breed is the fact that fawn and brown are very often not distinguishable. I have always followed Mrs. Willison's advice only to mate three colours fawn, brown and blue with a born black. This ensures that good pigment and eye colour would also be well established within the breeding.

Picture of the whole Peewit House, Stotfold

The lounge at Peewit House

A friend drew this picture of Felix at her farm running away from the cows

Felix with all our prize cards at Peewit House

I know I have been accused of living in the past as my remarks and observations do not reflect the modern day Beardie. When I notice scissored feet, sculptured muzzle, eyes and ears, the long silky coat with unnatural parting from nose to tail, emphasising the drop behind the withers and the rise over the loin. I ask myself what next will be done to alter the breed. The standard says no scissoring is allowed but when I am judging and remark on scissored feet, I am told the dog runs on pebbles which make the feet look as if it had been scissored. What has happened to the animation that is called for, the far seeing beautiful expression has also in my opinion been lost, and then I noticed the next Beardie that I am to judge has a wagging tail, no parting, natural hair growth with good undercoat. Then on the move with a loose lead the dog has sound free action, I think to myself all is not lost there are a few real Bearded Collies left.

At the Beagold Kennels we had some excellent quality built kennels, each dog had their own sleeping quarters and a good size run. We also had a large grass area for the dogs to exercise and play with each other. The most important room when you own Bearded Collies is a grooming room. I spent hours in this room mainly because Felix was not a keen groomer. We saw that the Breed was being over glamorised and neither of us were in love with spending hours in the grooming room so we started looking for another breed similar to the character of the Bearded Collie in the early days.

Felix Cosme and Tilehouse Cassius at Beagold receives the first Dog CC in 1982 from Mrs Catherine Sutton at Crufts where Mr Eric Broadhurst won the first Bitch CC with Sh. Ch. Tracelyn Gal (Photo: Frank Garwood)

Cassius awarded his 3rd CC

A NEW LOVE WITH THE BORDER COLLIE

THE TV program "One man and his dog" attracted many of the dog people and first time owners to want a dog exactly like the working Border Collies on TV. The Border Collie was due to be accepted for the show ring by the Kennel Club. These were the dogs and bitches that were registered with the ISDS (International Sheepdog Society). They would be accepted for show after they were also registered with the Kennel Club. Both Felix and I had admired the breed for several years and we decided to search for every bit of information about the Border Collie.

I heard of a litter of Border Collie puppies bred by a well known breeder and I contacted her to book a puppy dog that I was planning to give to Felix as a birthday present, I had suggested that we were going to look at the litter, when we arrived the breeder pointed out the dog that she had held back for me to look at. I had told her that Felix was a keen Boxing fan, the breeder said that he was a tough little puppy and fought to be first at the teats. I then said "Felix that's your birthday present". Then Felix said, "We will call him Cassius".

When he matured, Cassius made breed history as his name sake did. Cassius was the first Border Collie to win a Challenge Certificate when the breed was first allocated Challenge Certificate at Crufts 1982. His second and third came soon after making him the first Show Champion in the breed.

We decided to add a Border Collie bitch to the kennels

in the hopes that we could produce puppies with his wonderful character and type.

There was a litter for sale at a farm in Northampton, so we went to view the pups. They were in a huge dark barn, and it was obvious they had not had any human contact other than the farmer when he brought in their food. I saw one well made puppy bitch and asked to see it closer. Sadly the farmer trod on the pup and it ran away behind a bail of straw. We decided the temperament of the litter was not good enough for our plans, on the way out of the barn we saw two Border Collies in a pig stye, I asked the farmer if the bitch was for sale, so he got the bitch out to show me. I was very impressed with her makeup so we bought her. We named her Destiny at Beagold.

I know there are many exhibitors and dog owners that started with their chosen breeds and continued throughout their show career dedicated to that one breed. I love all breeds, some more than others, they all have their own special characteristics whatever size, type and temperament. Throughout my dog owning career, I have been excited and keen to own nearly all breeds whatever group they fall in. I was able to add another breed to our kennels when our beloved pets passed away, I did not want to replace any of them, for there could never be another Cassius, Derhue or Bliss, or Bearded Collie Camerro.

I was judging Bouvier des Flandes at a championship show and I was taken with all of them as it is a very handsome breed. I wondered if there was room at our kennels for a Bouvier puppy for they had not so much coat in fact a completely different type of coat and one which I knew I could cope with.

Felix and I travelled to see a litter of Bouviers at Miranda Lucas (Sacul) at her home up north. I just had to give a home to the gorgeous black puppy she brought to show us and that is how Sacul Excelcior, pet name John Pierre

Destiny at Beagold. (Photo: Dave Freeman)

Joyce showing Sacul Excelcior Bouvier des Flandres at Crufts

joined the Beagold Kennels.

I was very upset when I got ill and the doctor told me that grooming dogs in a closed room with spray and powder had given me an infected throat so sadly we had to sell some of our pups and not replace the old ones when they died.

We decided that the Border Collie did not have a problem coat, and the temperament and working instinct in the breed was similar to what attracted us to the Bearded Collie before the show world decided the breed should be glamorised.

On our way to Bedford one day we saw a man disappearing into a field, he had two border Collies following close to his heel. In the field was a large flock of sheep. We stopped the car as soon as we could and ran into the field, but there was no sign of him. We had no idea where he had gone, but later we learnt that the man was Mr. Norman Seamark, a well known expert in Border Collie sheepwork training. Felix contacted him and asked if he could join the students to train his Border Collie dog Cassius. Mr. Seamark said he was organizing a class of six students and he would contact Felix when they fixed a date. Cassius was one year old and keen to join in any activity at that early stage. The years went by, and he heard nothing from Mr. Seamark. When later Felix met him at a show and asked him if he should continue waiting for his call, it would have to be a different dog though as Cassius died at the age of 13 years in 1991.

Our next journey made to add a Border Collie to join our family was to visit Mrs. Barbara Carpenter's farm in Wales. She had decided to part with a close relation of Ch. Brocken Sweep. She said Moss was a waste of time as he would not work, and seemed deaf to all instructions. That is how Moss came to live with us, and we showed him a few times, but we must admit he was a lazy dog. Felix had put an easy chair in his large kennel, and attached a tray to the arm, so that he could eat his food without getting out of his chair. He had the sweetest temperament and appreciated the comfort. After a while we went visiting Mrs. Carpenter again and took Moss with us. He remembered the farm so we allowed him to roam, and when we were not watching him he crept off and when we eventually found him, he was working the flock of sheep beautifully without human interference. Mrs. Carpenter could see that he had inherited the working instinct but she had already replaced him. She was quite happy for us to bring him back with us.

Poor Moss he did not live long. We returned from judg-

Joyce judging first Border Collie Club Show where her BIS was disqualified as one of the parents was unregistered

ing abroad and found him in a very bad state, the Vet told us that his kidneys had been affected and he would be in pain and gradually get worst as he had Leptospirosis. We left him with the Vet to put him peacefully to sleep.

I was very pleased to be invited to judge the Border Collie Club show of GB at Weedon, Northampton in 1980. I did not expect a large entry as we were right at the beginning of the Border Collie being accepted by the Kennel Club on their show register. There was a very large entry for the Obedience held on the same day as many of the dogs entered were working sheepdogs. I had a varied entry of many different types. My best in show was a beautifully made bitch, very feminine, sound in all quarters, and moved with a typical Border Collie gait. Sadly later she was disqualified from her win as the committee checked her pedigree and the sire had not been registered with the ISDS or the Kennel Club. There were several well made Border Collies at that time that did not have both parents registered, and could only be accepted for the Kennel Club working sheepdog register.

I was delighted to receive a judging appointment in New Zealand at their Club Championship Show. The Australian dog world had already booked me to judge at three shows in 1988 so they suggested that I combined my visit to both countries at the same time, so they could share my travel expenses.

As it got nearer the time for my journey I received a letter from both countries giving me the breeds I was contracted to judge. The only slight worry that I had was that this was going to be a long and tiring journey on my own.

Felix and I had always been keen to see the type of Border Collie in New Zealand and Australia which we had heard exhibitors talking about. We had decided if I saw a really good dog that pleased me I was to phone Felix telling him that the quality was as good as we had thought.

The journey to New Zealand took such a long time. Most judges who had made that journey went a different route to mine. I left Heathrow on Thursday, arrived in America, I think on Friday, and arrived in Auckland on Saturday Morning. I was met at the airport by a young man and taken to his home. On the journey he told me that there was a huge entry of Belgian Shepherds waiting for me to judge. I had no idea that I was contracted to judge the breed. Did he realize that I had been travelling for three days and I was very tired. We arrived at his home and I was introduced to his wife, there were owners and Belgian

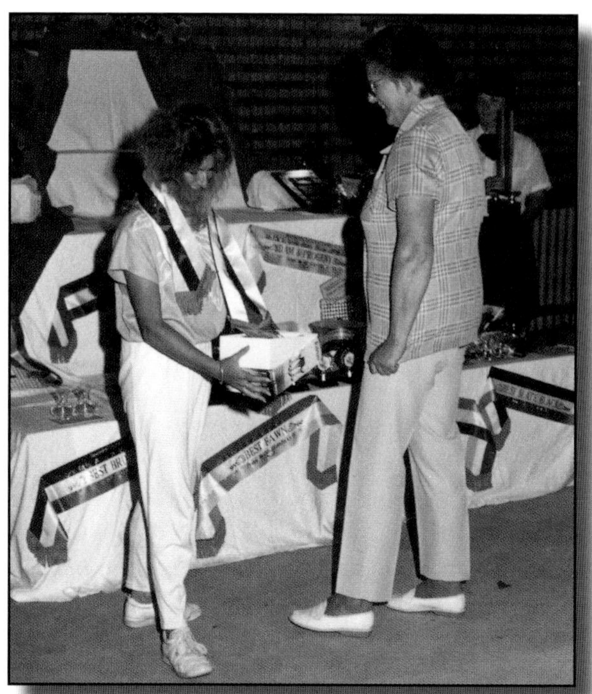

Joyce giving prizes to winners in Melbourne, Australia

Judging Belgium Shepherds in Sydney Australia

Shepherds everywhere. His wife suggested I had a cup of tea then rested for an hour on their bed. In the bedroom I noticed two cats had escaped from all the visitors and their dogs and were fast asleep on the bed. I took my shoes off and fell exhausted onto the bed. To my surprise I found the water bed sank with my weight, but bounced the cat up in the air. Where they went I did not care.

At eleven o'clock I was taken to the venue for the show. My excited host introduced me to the Mayor of the town, and the exhibitors were already lined up in the ring so I started judging. I had been given an invitation to judge and give a lecture in New Zealand, by the Border Collie Club, before I went to Australia. This extra judging appointment had not been mentioned. I knew that the various clubs in order to cut down their travelling cost of visiting judges, would farm out to other clubs the judges they had originally contacted. In other words the Border Collie Club in New Zealand and the other Clubs in Australia would share my expenses of travel and accommodation. But it was obvious that they had overlooked this Belgian Shepherd appointment. A lot of work had gone into the preparation of this show, everything was set up perfectly, cups and trophies and the rings were set out correctly. I finished judging and presented the trophies to the winners, and thought I could now retire, I was wrong, they had organized a barbecue for that evening, and I was guest of honour.

Eventually I went to bed at midnight. I was then told to be up early as my host was taking me to another part of Auckland to the Border Collie Championship show, where I was to be the only judge.

When I arrived at my new destination I was informed that I was to judge that day, I told them that it was a bit much for me to travel all that distance and be judging at two shows in two days. They were shocked as this was completely news to them, and as the man who dropped me off dashed away they could not question him on the details. But they assured me that they would be investigating the situation. I had been informed that it never rained in New Zealand at that time of year so I did not go prepared when low and behold it started to rain all day. I was loaned a small plastic mac as there was no wet weather accommodation.

Next day it was a beautiful sunny day and I was taken to many homes where I saw some beautiful scenery. Yellow budgerigars flew over one house and landed in their tree, making it look like green and golden flowers in bloom. Beside the road, Lilies and Azaleas bloomed like wild flowers. I had a judging appointment in Australia so after five days I caught the plane to Sydney.

Everything was so different, especially at the airport. The official looked at me suspiciously as he checked my passport and asked me what I was doing in New Zealand as I had stayed there for only 5 days. I told him that I was judging. He queried, "At which court were you judging?". I answered, "Not a court, but a dog show in Auckland." His mannerism changed completely as soon as I had mentioned a dog show and I went on to tell him that I had judged in many countries, but this was my first appointment in New Zealand and Australia. I was not surprised when he asked, "Have you judged at Crufts?" to which I replied that I had.

He then asked me if I could come back the next day ,when he would arrange for me to see their search dogs working in the airport to find drugs. I was delighted and pleased to accept, the friend that was meeting me was writing a book on dogs, and wanted to include the working Police and Air Force dogs. Next day we arrived at the gates and were welcomed in to watch the Labradors working in a huge hanger, it was a wonderful sight.

There were hundreds of cases, trunks, and a variety of suitcases all stacked up to the rafters. I could not imagine how any dog even if as agile as a monkey could search for the decoy, as it would mean he had to jump and scramble up impossible heights with very little footing.

We watched spellbound, then the Labrador gave a loud bark and knocked a case down to the floor below. He scratched at the case then the policeman told him to leave it, so the dog backed away and sat down. The policeman opened the case to find another suitcase inside it, he then found a bottle inside the suitcase which he opened and showed us several pills. The Labrador watched us, then the policeman took out a green ball from his pocket and gave it to the excited dog. This was his favourite ball, and obviously with all the work he had done to find the drugs he would be rewarded with that favourite ball.

During the years that followed I had the most exciting life travelling to so many different countries. In Zimbabwe I was not aware that I had to pay ten American dollars to the officials before I left the Airport. So many people came to welcome me, and no one thought to mention it. The next day Karen Peel, my hostess, in casual conversation said, "You did pay your ten dollars before you left the Airport?" She was very worried when I said that I had not paid. We had to go straight to the Government offices in town to pay them.

We arrived at a very large building, with black uniformed guards at every door. We were directed to a long corridor and told to wait. We were sent to an office, behind the desk was a huge Blackman in uniform laden down with medals and gold braid.

I am not afraid to say I was frightened. I had the ten dollars ready in my shaking hand. The official was delighted to have two nervous white women in his clutches and gave us a lecture, emphasising the fact that I had purposely kept the ten dollars back.

I apologised profusely and said I was so pleased to come

to Zimbabwe to judge at their show that I had forgotten their rules. He took the ten dollars and warned me that I should be more honest next time I came. I felt like telling him that there was no chance I would be returning but I said nothing and we left.

Karen was so kind she took me sightseeing several times. Once we went to a Crocodile farm. A fascinating place where I saw the Crocodile eggs under a lamp on one table and on the next table I saw the baby Crocs eating their way out of the eggs, from then on they were in another room that was full of small ponds. The ponds and Crocs got larger as they grew.

We also went on a shopping trip to Harare. As she parked the car there was a noisy uproar, a huge armoured car and a small tank came into the carpark, two soldiers jumped out of their car and another took his place on the tank and setup a machine gun at the ready. The two soldiers carried two heavy sacks into the bank. Everyone backed away, some people left quickly and I was warned to stay in our car with the windows shut, I had no intention of moving until Karen came back. She was unperturbed and told me that happens every week, she should have warned me.

The next day I was taken to the show set out exactly like we have here, everything went smoothly. I started doing my breeds and found the Border Collies were super as they were mainly dogs that had all the freedom they needed. Best of Breed I gave to Mr. and Mrs. Portch's Border Collie Ch. Inemar Taff. Best In Show went to a Boxer.

It was time to leave Zimbabwe, I sat in the Airport waiting room with a lot of passengers waiting to be called. I had left my friends and felt very lonely. The first batch of passengers were called and left the room. The second batch were called which worried me very much as I was left behind with the two young Missionaries. I wondered why they had been chosen to be left, and thought I had been left because I had been slow paying my ten dollars to the

Judging in Zimbabwe Africa

My winner when judging in Zimbabwe Africa

Government, surely the country could not have been that hard up. The two Missionaries did not speak English so I had no chance of asking them anything. One of the staff came into the room and told us to follow him. Imagine my surprise when he escorted us to the plane, and told us to sit in the first class seat. It seemed that they had no other first class paying passengers so they were free to the two Missionaries and Joyce Collis who was the judge for the dog show.

My next visit abroad was the following year to South Africa again, one of the shows I was to judge was the Collie Club show of Johannesburg which included Rough, Smooth and Border Collies. I was to stay at the home of our friends Ron and Vanessa Juckes. Their house was huge with a swimming pool and a large garden surrounding the property.

I was a little disappointed with the quality of the Rough Collies that I judged first, it was a large entry but the presentation was not good. The owners had made this show their own, they had set up tents, caravans and cars around the ring. I was told that every year they won most of the trophies, and this would certainly be another successful year as I was a specialist judge for Rough Collies from GB. They had already been celebrating as I had finished judging the small Smooth Collie entry.

They were very surprised to see the very large entry of Border Collies, many had travelled from Harare with their youngsters and Champions. When I had finished judging the Border Collies I had to judge the Best Puppy, Best Junior, Best Open and CC winner from the three breeds. That was when the trouble started. When I gave Best Puppy in Show to the Border Collie they definitely made their annoyance felt. My choice for Best In Show went to the Border Collie it was obvious that their celebrating drinks was the excuse to shout even louder. The Secretary called in the President of the South African Kennel Union. He was in complete agreement with my placings and apologized for the behaviour of the Rough Collie exhibitors. I decided then and there that although Africa was a beautiful country I was now satisfied with my two visits and did not need a third. After the show I was told that the reason the President was called in was because the secretary, unknown to me was the owner of the dog that was my choice for Best Rough Collie and several exhibitors were highly annoyed with the secretary for even entering his dog.

I have mentioned the first time I went to America to judge Bearded Collies before they were accepted for showing in that country. The next visit was a few years later to judge at the bearded Collie Club of America. A huge entry of over 200 dogs awaited me.

I had not told my brother Peter and his wife I was coming to America as it was to be a short visit. I was very surprised when an unknown lady and her husband rushed into the ring to welcome me, and asked why I had not told my brother that I was in America. She explained to me that we had met at my last visit to my brother's house in Philadelphia.

Felix was manager and joint owner of the Beagold Kennels, so I was free to accept judging appointments abroad. I was pleased that he had started judging which enabled him to keep me company during my travels.

My third visit to America, was with Felix and it made such a difference to have company. We put the dogs in Boarding Kennels, and were able to make a longer stay in America and he was able to take me to visit some of his friends.

I had to go alone for my judging appointment to Gibraltar. I found it all so political when the British that worked in Gibraltar but lived in Spain, had to travel through a police barrier to get home. The venue for the show was in the Gibraltar airfield. I was staying with friends who lived in Spain and they took me to the show, as we arrived at the show early they took me through miles and miles of underground passageways in the Rock of Gibraltar. A fascinating place, as soldiers in their hundreds lived there during the second world war.

I was pleased to go with Felix to Norway to judge and we stayed with friends in Trondheim. The day of the show I was introduced to a man who owned a German Shepherd Dog, he explained to me and my Norwegian friend that it was so vicious that no one could touch or handle it, so he intended to have it put down before it bit anyone again. I told him that Felix was very good with German Shepherd Dogs and would be sure to train the dog, as I had seen him tame several dogs with his clever methods.

Next day the man came to our friends house with his dog, I had not told Felix that the dog was untrainable and vicious. When he saw the dog, he said, “Let me see if I can show train it.” I noticed that he patted the dog on the head before he took it outside into the garden. We all dashed to the window to watch Felix and the dog. We were amazed that the dog showed no aggression to him at all as he went through the ritual of the show ring. The owner could not believe his eyes as he watched his aggressive bad tempered dog submit to firm and kind handling by Felix. The owner started crying and he said through his tears “I cannot believe it, I cannot believe it.” When Felix entered the room with the dog we all started clapping and then I told him the truth about the dog’s character.

I have just related to you the serious and exciting life one leads in the world of dog showing. The final chapters will allow you to realize that there is a most amusing and comical side of the dog showing world as well.

When I look back over the many years that I have been involved with puppies, dog showing, and judging, I realize that it has been a very enjoyable part of my life. I was very lucky to meet Felix, a person with the same interest

Best in Show
Norway 1979

Judging in Norway

At Crufts with Bernese Mountain Dog

Judging a Belgium Shepherd in Scotland

as mine. He managed the kennels while I was free to travel abroad to judge. At first he was only interested in handling our dogs, but he then took on judging as well.

We started to realize that we were getting tired of kennel work, and showing our own dogs. If we wanted to carry on judging we would have to cut down some of our activities.

With the two dogs that we had, we could move to a smaller home with less ground and nearer to town. We would not need so many kennels, and it would be less expensive to board our two dogs when travelling together.

My husband George had passed away fifteen years ago, so as we would be living together in a smaller house, we decided to get married on 1st November 2007.

When we decided to sell the Beagold kennels at Peewit house we had many enquiries, which we found unsuitable. We decided what would be an ideal situation was for us to exchange houses with a friend who wanted more space and fourteen rooms to cope with. To this day neither Felix nor have I regretted the move to our present address in town.

We still judge a few times a year, both here and abroad.

Judging in Holland and Felix came to visit 1978

Felix with Ch Castleavery Sylvester winning Best in Show

In such a comfortable home that we now have we enjoy our semi retirement, with just two Swedish Vallhunds, Sylvester and Granville to look after.

I was so pleased when I was invited recently to a reception at County Hall, Hartford by Dione the Countess of Verulem, Lord Lieutenant of Hertfordshire and the Councillor Cllr. Nigel Brook, when the Womens Land Army were honoured at a special meeting. We were all given a certificate of service and a medal, which I will certainly treasure.

In the local newspaper we were also honoured with an article headed SALUTE TO WOMEN WHO DUG FOR VIC-

Litter of Swedish Vallhunds

Me handling Swedish Vallhund Sylvester at Bedford Open Show

Womens Landarmy in Horse & Cart, girls in working uniform, Land Army Celebration, Hertfordshire 1st March 2008

Reception with myself and the other women being photographed at the Land Army Celebration, Hertfordshire 1st March 2008

5 - COMET, March 5, 2009 www.thecomet24.co.uk

Comet *News* advertising 01438 866075 news 01438 866200 web www.thecomet24.co.uk

Salute to women who dug for victory

TWO women who served in the Women's Land Army and Timber Corps during World War II were honoured at a special reception last week.

Joyce Cosme of Church Road, Stotfold, and Gladys Levett of The Lawns, Stevenage, were among 250 former land girls at a reception held at County Hall, Hertford, as guests of Hertfordshire County Council.

There they met Dione the Countess of Verulam and Lord Lieutenant of Hertfordshire and the chairman of the council Cllr Nigel Brook from St Ippolyts.

Joyce, now in her 80s, joined the Women's Land Army when she was 17 after she tried to join the armed forces but was told she needed to be 18.

During the war she was evacuated to Bournemouth from the family home in Wanstead Park in London and was soon working at a farm on the Hampshire Downs.

But working with the animals was often far from mundane as she recalled one morning she will never forget.

"I had gone out to the chickens to collect the eggs," said Joyce.

"When I stuck my head inside the hen-house I saw a German officer eating raw eggs.

"I said 'hello' and ran. He had parachuted down safely after his aircraft had been hit. The previous night two aircraft had crashed near the farm.

"He must have been very hungry and the police came and took him away and I never saw him again."

Joyce Cosme with her medal and certificate (right) and (above) as a Land Army girl ***AM09land2***

Joyce also remembers one Christmas when she was riding her bicycle and fell off on a slippery road and slid under a lorry breaking her arm.

"I was lucky not to be killed, but young women worked so hard on the land to help with the war effort," added Joyce.

Mrs Levett, 83, who has lived in Stevenage for 50 years, was living in the family home in Old Kent Road, London, when she volunteered for the Land Army.

"I didn't want to work in a munitions factory so I joined the Land Army and went to work on a farm near Petworth in Sussex," said Gladys.

"We had wonderful times and I was at a farm for three years as a milk maid until the war ended.

"We didn't see any action but I remember one very clear and light night looking up and seeing something coming out of a plane. At first I thought it was a bomb but then realised it was a parachute.

"We had some wonderful young Canadians staying nearby and I made a lot of friends and then, when the war was over, I moved back to London and got married. All this happened over 60 years ago but it was nice to be recognised for all the hard work Land Army girls did."

Two other women from Stevenage, Ruby Robinson and Doris Merry, who served in the Land Army, also attended the event.

Gladys Levett with her service medal and (left) pictured during her time with the Women's Land Army (below) ***AM09gladys1***

Medal from Womens Land Army

Certificate from Prime Minister Gordon Brown

TORY. It was also a very sad occasion for me as many of the Land Army girls were in wheel chairs, many needed assistance to walk, and it was obvious to me as we were so few in number that many had passed away.

As I mentioned before, the next chapter will enable you the readers to realize that there is also a very amusing side to dog showing and judging.

AND FINALLY SOME AMUSING TAILS

RIGHT in the middle of the Parvo Virus scare I was asked why I did not put up a very sad looking West Highland White in the class. The poor little dog had drooped around the ring, it seemed to have no life left, and squatted down by my judge's table and passed a long stream of pink liquid. The owner quickly covered the mess up with her foot and said, "There is nothing wrong with this dog, it is just the heat," and she dragged the poor dog out of the ring.

Such sad situations are very upsetting, and as a dog lover it is hard for me to see such neglect and cruelty and not shame the owner. Thank goodness there are a lot of very amusing incidents in the dog world as well.

Judges use the dog show language that sometimes is not understood by the novice and many misunderstandings can cause embarrassment to the exhibitor. My policy has been the same right from the start of my judging career, that is to forget who is holding the lead of their dog and have eyes only for the exhibit. I was giving a CC in a breed that I was judging at a show up North. My CC and BOB dog, and my CC winning bitch were standing with me to have our photo taken. The lady who owned the BOB dog said to me, "I am so surprised Joyce, that you have put me up, I thought you did not like me at all." I answered her, "I do not like you and I never have, but I was judging dogs not people". I have continued with that policy throughout my career. People who were present on that day and heard what I had said still remind me today of it.

When I judged in Sydney and Melbourne in Australia I remember so many amusing incidents. While in Sydney, during my appointment I heard shouting and people running away in panic when a fire was noticed burning in the woods nearby. Nearly everyone dashed to help put the fire out as the woods had so many eucalyptus trees burning, this could extend into a bush fire for miles, devastating the country, animals and houses. If this had happened in England I am sure the English exhibitors would have waited to see who won the CC and BOB. I heard later that the fire was started by a lady who had found the dead body of a fox in her garden, she tried to bury it but the ground was too hard and dry, so she poured petrol over the carcass and the flames soon spread and could have caused a bush fire.

It was very difficult to get to Melbourne as there was an aeroplane strike and there was no chance that the strike would be over by the end of the week for me to get there in time to judge, so they asked me if I would agree to travel to Melbourne in a Chookie Lorry (chicken delivery lorry). I was none to pleased about the thought of a long journey in an uncomfortable lorry, so was delighted to learn that a committee member agreed to fly me down in his private plane.

Most of my judging appointments abroad in those days included a request for me to give lecture of the breeds that I was to judge. After I had judged Border Collies in Zimbabwe and had given my talk, during the following question time I was asked why I made it clear that I preferred the Border Collies with a flat top coat and plenty of undercoats, as I had penalised the dogs with curly coats. I explained that the Border Collie, especially in England had to go out to work in all sorts of weather, the rain would run off the flat coated types, but would

Newspaper men took this photo of Bernie 1970. He was the first Bernese Mountain Dog to qualify for Crufts. (Photo: Reg Denton)

get into the body of the curly coated ones. A lady in the audience asked, "Please explain what rain is, as we have had a drought for the past five years". This caused hilarious laughter. I felt a bit foolish as in England we never have a drought.

When we had Border Collies a lady telephoned to ask if our dogs were at stud. I enquired if her bitch had been tested for HD, and if she had been checked for CEA. She replied that she had not bothered but she did know that the sire and dam had both produced CEA but not HD in their previous litter. I told her that I was sorry, but she really should not mate the bitch with that history of abnormalities. She mentioned that I had written in one of my books, that if anyone doubted that the bitch was clear of those problems, they should go to a reputable kennels and use a stud dog that was clear. I explained to her that the problems I had mentioned were slight show problems, like not enough under coat, show markings, temperaments etc, certainly not health problems like CEA and HD. In fact her bitch should not be mated, as the resulting litter could carry those genes.

Throughout all our many years in dogs we have had so many funny calls from novice dog owners. One lady phoned to tell me that her dog was mounting her little boy, and she took it to the Vet. He advised her to have the dog castrated, she agreed to have it done. Sadly it did not alter the dog's behaviour, so at her next visit the Vet advised her to have the dog's dew claws removed, she also agreed. The situation did not alter, rather annoyed and badly out of pocket when the dog's behaviour continued she thought it best to contact me as the Vet had advised her to have the dog's teeth removed. I suggested she change her Vet and find a new home for the dog as he was highly sexed and certainly should not be around young children. I would have put him down immediately.

There are so many would be dog owners who do not have the slightest knowledge of what owning a dog entails, especially if they have young children. Having a family of young children should take up all their spare time anyway. When we have a litter for sale and a buyer comes to view the Pups I always ask so many questions about their situation at home and would a young pup, a lively young pup fit in with their lives.

A middle aged couple came to view our litter of pups and having asked all the relevant questions I was so pleased with their answers that we both agreed here was the ideal home. Imagine our shock when they phoned when the pup was just over four months old to ask if we would have the puppy back, they loved him, he was a healthy beautiful pup, but their gardener was complaining he chewed the plants and lifted his leg on the roses. That was the one question we did not ask, "Did they have a beautiful garden, and a fussy gardener?"

At Llandudno in January 1989 I was judging Corgis, and a very nice Corgi bitch handled by a lady came for assessment. When I asked her age I was not sure what the lady said, when she spoke to her bitch I did not understand again what she said. Later I gave her BOB and found we had not got a BOB rosette, so I told her to go to the Secretary's table to get her BOB rosette, she seemed confused as if she did not understand me, so I asked her, "Are you a foreign lady?" She looked hurt and said to me, "No I am Welsh".

I was judging at a show near London, and I had been warned that the Secretary was never around when the luncheon vouchers were given to the judges. This being a regular occurrence I decided that as I had a lot of breeds and classes to judge, I would make sure I got a luncheon voucher. I called at the Secretary's desk for my judging book, prize cards etc. when I arrived at 10am. Then I said, "Also can I have my luncheon vouchers now please". She snapped back at me, “What are you hungry already”.

We have met so many different characters in the dog world that I am never surprised when I meet another. We were very sad to learn that a very well known breeder of gundogs had died. Many of his friends wanted to show respect and help his wife at his funeral. A friend who lived near her arranged for the funeral car with his coffin to go from his house. We all met in our cars and waited for the wife to arrive. Imagine our surprise when we saw her come out of her house to put two of her dogs in her car. She was dressed in her dog show clothes and called out to all of us that she was ready to go to the cemetery and thanked us all for coming, she was going on from the church to a dog show. After the church service the Vicar had spoken to her and asked what she wanted done with her husband’s ashes. She said she was going to a dog show and could not take them, so would he keep them until she got back.

Felix and I travelled abroad to give a talk at a show handling training, this was to give advice and help to very novice owners. Felix went out on the field with half the trainees and I worked hard all day with the other half. I was very pleased by the evening I could see a marked improvement in my trainees. Leads were held loosely and encouragement was given to the shy dogs. Strong commands not requests were given to the unruly dogs. When the dogs came into the ring at first they behaved unruly and I imagined it would take more than one day to see any improvement. I was wrong, most of the dogs moved correctly, especially the Border Collies who moved with their tails down and head level with their back. I was delighted with my success in training the owners I thanked them all and dismissed the class. I glanced out of the door as they left the hall and to my horror I saw tight leads, heads strung up like terriers and tails curled over the backs as they jumped around as if none of my training had been taken notice of, Felix had a slightly better response.

The Kennel Club rules for the Miniature Dachshund is that it should be weighed in the show ring and must not weigh more than 11 lbs. I was watching a very plump lady lift her dog onto the scales and saw her look of surprise when the scales dropped heavily indicating the dog was well overweight. She looked horrified more than likely knowing that her little dog was the correct weight when she left home. The judge went forward and said to the lady in a quiet voice, "Stand back madam it is you that pushed the weight of the scale down with your bust and not your dog." She stood back away from the scales and her dog was under the required 11 lbs.

I was judging gundogs at a show in Hampshire, some of the rings were outdoor and some were inside the hall, as it was threatening to rain I decided to judge inside, three young female exhibitors immediately complained that they wanted to be judged outside even as the rain fell. I told them they could be in the ring for a few minutes but I would have to stand out in the rain for all the classes. They gave in. One surly young lady said, "My dog does not like not like to move towards a corner". I told her she had to try. It was true as the dog stopped half way. "I told you she did not like to go towards corners". I said try the other corner. The dog again refused and stopped. She smiled and said, "Can we now go outside?" I smiled sweetly back at her and said, "Take your dog straight across the ring as there are no corners in that direction". The dog went straight across and back showing very nice movement, much to her owner's annoyance.

At this show a taxi driver drew up and a lady struggled out but left the taxi driver to get her four Rough Collies out. He was not a happy man, the dogs had all messed in his taxi. The owner took them from him and asked the Secretary of the show to get someone to help the taxi driver to clean up the mess. He had not been paid so set about cleaning the floor of his taxi. The Chairman of the show ran out to speak to the lady and reminded her that she had been banned from this show, so he advised her to get back into the taxi and return home, and not to come to his show again. All this 'to do' had attracted a large audience. By this time the taxi mess had been cleaned up, and the driver was asking for his money. He did not look happy when he was told he had to drive the lady and her four Collies home before she would pay him. Everyone admired his patience.

While watching the group at another show I was told that this present judge in the ring had short listed 8 dogs for the group. The judge moved the dogs again, again, and again, and then stood and stared at them before choosing the 1st, 2nd, 3rd, and 4th he was so unsure of his placings that a voice from outside the ring shouted, "What's the matter do you have too many friends and not enough places?"

I was judging a dog belonging to an elderly man who obviously had a shaking illness. He held his dog on a very tight lead and the dog leaned closely against him. As I went over to the dog he said to me, "My Labrador is always shaking like that." I could see that the man had the problem so I said to him, "Stand back and hold your dog on a very loose lead". He stood away from his dog and was amazed that the Labrador had stopped shaking. I asked him to move his dog up and down the ring, he tightened the lead again, bent low over the dog, and both of them went up the ring shaking. I called him back and told him to move with a loose lead again and move away from his dog. The dog moved perfectly. Later the owner came up to me and thanked me profusely, telling me his dog had stopped shaking and for the first time moved properly on a loose lead. As he walked away I saw he was shaking. But the dog was breathing a sigh of relief and walked normally.

A lady brought her bitch to be mated to one of our Champions. When we saw the bitch we were not happy with her looks, although she had quite a good pedigree. We noticed many faults which would hold her back from ever winning in the show ring. The owner told us she had no intentions of showing her, but if she used a Champion it would be easy to sell the puppies. She asked what the stud fee was and we told her it would be one hundred pounds, which was then the price we had charged for a puppy. She said, "I will charge one hundred and fifty pounds." I suggested that she charged the same as we did, even less as her bitch was not show quality, also she was not known in the show world and would have problems selling her pups. Her answer was, "I am sure I will sell all the pups as I am using your Champion, regardless of how bad my bitch looks." We advised her to try elsewhere for a stud service.

We had an enquiry for a puppy that would win at Championship shows like Crufts, and if they had time they wanted to work sheep as a Border Collie must be trained to work sheep. The owners would pay for it to be trained, and would always have it groomed professionally. Another important point, they wanted a dog that could live in the house, definitely not a furniture chewer, and certainly a dog that would not frighten the grand children. When it gets older it must not bark, or never mess or mark its territory in the house. My suggestion to the lady was to buy a china ornament of a dog.

I was judging abroad and one of the breeds I had was Rough Collies. When the judging was completed the exhibitor returned to ask me why I had not placed his Rough Collie dog, and why I did not like his dog. I told him I found the other dogs complied better with the standard. He told me that last week he had shown his dog in Belgium and he won the CACIB and BOB. I was then forced to tell him that I personally found the dog's head too deep, the eyes too round, and the dog was quite noticeably cowhocked. "That should not matter, it should not make all that much difference, he was like that last week and he still won".

It is not only me that encounters strange situations that are amusing, for example my husband Felix was judging Junior Handling Classes. A little boy 9 years old was having trouble settling his dog in the ring. He was asked the dog's age which he did not know, Felix then said to him, "Don't worry, just show me the teeth", then the little boy stood up from his dog and showed his own teeth with a lovely smile. Obviously the little boy did not realise it was the dog's teeth that needed to be shown.

Once you have chosen to be involved in the fascinating hobby of owning dogs, breeding litters and judging, it can involve travelling all over the world to attend dog shows, it is a hobby and a way of life impossible to give up easily.

We have often said to each other, we will only have one more litter, they grow up and leave then we say, "We have champions in the making so for the good of the breed should have one more litter". Judging dogs is also a hobby hard to give up. We are invited to see the world with very little expense, so long as we know all the breeds that we are contracted to judge. I personally have never accepted a judging appointment here or abroad, without having the confidence, experience, and knowledge of the breed that I will judge. It is only with over forty years of judging that I have gained this experience.

My interest is to judge the natural dog, that is built correctly, well muscled, sound in construction for the work he or she will be called upon to do for the working breeds. The terrier should also be in the condition to attend to what he was bred for. The Toy is a companion and pet, so temperament is the main criteria. The hound needs to be in prime condition and construction, also well muscled even if it is only to be used in the show ring.

I do not favour excessive artificially presented dogs. There is a chance that the best cosmetic presentation like the Poodle ,Wire Fox Terrier, Kerry Terrier, etc, and now the Bearded Collie will win over natural presentation. The Bearded Collie was a working dog, out in all weathers working over all sorts of ground, needing a harsh coat, and the harsh correct coat does not grow so long as the long silky coat now seen so often in the show ring.

When judging I start by accessing the head, then I ask to see the mouth (the bite), and have had so often, the owner bending over to look at the dog's mouth at the same time. I sometimes say, "You have seen the bite, now let me look at it".

I have asked to see the bite in the Pekingese and have been told, "You do not look in the mouth of a Peke". I ask if it has got teeth, the answer is, "Of course it has," I then tell them, "I want to see them". I have even had owners withdraw their dogs from the showing, but professional owners agree that the teeth can be looked at.

I received a telephone call from the Irish Kennel Club, asking me if I was free to judge several breeds at their St. Patrick's Day championship Show. I said, "I would like to judge for you but what is the date?" He sounded shocked and said, "Everybody knows the date of the St. Patrick's Day celebration." I then realized I had made a fauxpas. So I said, "Of course I know the date and will be pleased to judge for you". I quickly looked up the date to see if I was free.

Some judges are very keen to sit at the Top Table at the special dinners held on the first night of a show, where all the celebrities sit. A well know judge, Harry Jordan no longer with us, came into the hall and asked me if I knew which end was the Top Table, I had no idea, and I really was not bothered. He said to me, "You must be sitting at the Top Table so I will leave my coat and case with you." I knew the Chairman, and he called me to sit with him and his wife at the other end of the hall. Everyone had arrived and to Harry's disgust there was only room for him with his coat and case at the bottom table on his own.

The Chairman was making his rounds to welcome everybody to their ring before they started judging, to thank the judges for coming to the Luxembourg Show. As had happened so often before, I had been allocated two Stewards who did not speak one word of English, and I was having trouble with them. The Chairman came to my ring and said, "Hello Mrs Collis is everything alright?" I replied, "No everything is not alright, could I have a Steward that speaks or understands English?" He smiled at me and said, "I am very pleased, thank you" and he left to go to the next ring. Obviously those were the only English words he had learnt just for these occasions.

Way back in the early days when I was exhibiting Bearded Collies I was so pleased to win a Challenge Certificate (CC) with my dog. The judge came forward to shake my hand and give me the Certificate, when I received a heavy blow on the back of my head, I am tall, but a short exhibitor had jumped up to hit me on the back of my head with her hair brush, she shouted out " I wanted that CC, you did not deserve it". The Judge jumped back thinking he was to receive the next blow from the exhibitor and said, "What nasty people you have in this breed." That lady is no longer with us.

When Felix and I got married we decided to make our Wills. We went to an old fashioned solicitor to record our wishes. We received copies to check that everything was in order and we were very surprised to read in Felix's Will, that, "When Felix Cosme passes away, his Estate will go to Felix Cosme". We went back to the Solicitor's Office and asked him, "What secret does he have about Death ,that we did not know about". He apologized and said he would rewrite the Will.

I am like most English judges when judging abroad I do not speak any language but my own. I hope the exhibitors understand me. The trouble is that I am allocated stewards that have the same problem. My two stewards were very helpful in many ways, but when it came for me to dictate my report on each dog we had language difficulties again. I had a very nice young dog that I had placed first. I dictated, "Excellent quality junior dog, immature but entire". I tried to explain that it was still a junior so had not matured in every aspect. She continued to look at me completely puzzled. I thought it best to tell her that it is like little boys that grow into adults and have testicles. She still did not understand what I was talking about. So I drew on a piece of paper two circles, she looked at the paper and said "I understand, I understand spectacles", she drew in the bridge over the nose, and the two arms that go over the ears. I said to her, "No not spectacles but testicles". She then seemed to understand. I have always written a list of names for every part of a dog that I am judging, and as she will have to interpret my dictation for the critique. Descriptive words like pasterns, stifle, topline, muzzle, shoulder, skull, dome, croup, will now definitely have the word testicles added to my list.

A very well dressed lady carried her Wire Haired Fox terrier into the ring, when it was her turn she placed her dog on the table for me to judge it. I went over it, then asked her if she would take her dog down the ring in a triangle, she lifted the dog off the table and carried it down the first part of the triangle, I called her back and said, "I want to see your dog's movement and you carried it all the way" she spoke back to me in a cross voice, "You did not tell me you wanted to see the dog's movement".

I would have thought it was obvious.

Felix and I were on our first judging appointment in the Czech Republic, we arrived at the crowded Airport searching for the people or person who was to pick us up and take us to our Hotel. This is a usual practice when they bring a card with our names printed on it, or a picture of the main breeds we are to judge. We hoped when the huge crowd dispersed we would see someone looking for us. Suddenly we saw a Bearded Collie dragging its lead on the ground coming straight towards us, followed by its owner trying to get through the crowd. It started wagging its tail, we could not believe our eyes in that crowded Airport how did that dog smell us out. We had never been to the Czech Republic before, and we had no connection with the dog. It will always amaze me how dogs can be so clever with their nose.

When I judged Rottweilers in S.Africa before the show I was taken to visit my hostess's friends. I arrived at each house where the house and grounds were surrounded by ten foot walls topped with barbwire. The dogs that came to the gate would frighten an Army of robbers. The Rottweilers were put away before we went in. At the show next day I was not so excited to learn that the Rottweiler entry was nearly one hundred. The show tent was beautifully decorated with the table full of cups, trophy and flowers. I was in the middle of my chosen hobby it was a pleasure to go over these handsome dogs, not one aggressive behaviour amongst them everything went smoothly. I enjoyed every minute. When I presented the prizes a lady said to me some judges are nervous when they judge our breed and you did not seem the slightest bit worried. My secret is I wash my hands in strong expensive perfume and it seems the dogs love it

It is so sad when a judge has spent a life time breeding, exhibiting, and judging dogs and has to retire. It is a life time of marvellous pleasure for the person who is a dedicated animal lover. I know I am one of those people, and when I meet another after just a little conversation I recognize I have met a kindred spirit. We push to the back of our minds that a time will come when we cannot continue with our chosen way of life.

SO, FINALLY, FINALLY, When is it Time to Retire

I was with an elderly lady who was at the show she had been called in to take the place of the scheduled group judge who had died. She had spent her whole life with dogs but had retired recently. The group judging had started she was introduced, I could see she was confused as more dogs arrived into the ring, she forgot to move the dogs she had already examined, and went to the dogs that had recently arrived. The exhibitors started slow hand clapping, and even allowed their dogs to lay down in the ring.

She looked lost and to my embarrassment she left the ring and came over to me, where I was sitting with the other judges and said in a loud voice, "Where ever do they think they are? At a football match. I have never seen such bad behaviour". She went back in the ring to continue judging, she had forgotten which dogs she had judged, it was chaos. One very well known, sympathetic gentlemanly judge went into the ring to speak to her. She followed him as he went back to his chair and came to me and said in a loud voice, "Joyce who does that man think he is telling me how to judge". She went back into the ring and finished the best she could.

This is a situation that we judges as we grow older must really know when it is the time to retire with our fond memories.